Shakespeare's

WORLD
of
LOVE

D0911437

THE DIRECTOR'S SHAKESPEARE SERIES
by Richard Courtney

SHAKESPEARE'S WORLD OF WAR
Henry VI, Parts 1, 2 & 3, Richard III, King John, Titus Andronicus

SHAKESPEARE'S COMIC WORLD
The Comedy of Errors, The Taming of the Shrew, The Two Gentlemen of Verona, Love's Labour's Lost, A Midsummer Night's Dream, The Merchant of Venice

SHAKESPEARE'S WORLD OF DEATH
Romeo and Juliet, Julius Caesar, Hamlet

SHAKESPEARE'S WORLD OF LOVE
Much Ado About Nothing, As You Like It, Twelfth Night, The Merry Wives of Windsor

SHAKESPEARE'S MASKED WORLD
Richard II, Henry IV, Parts 1 & 2, Henry V

SHAKESPEARE'S PROBLEM WORLD
All's Well That Ends Well, Measure for Measure, Troilus and Cressida, Timon of Athens, Coriolanus

SHAKESPEARE'S TRAGIC WORLD
Antony and Cleopatra, Macbeth, Othello, King Lear

SHAKESPEARE'S MAGIC WORLD
Pericles, Cymbeline, The Winter's Tale, The Tempest, Henry VIII, Two Noble Kinsmen

Shakespeare's

WORLD
of
LOVE

THE MIDDLE COMEDIES

Much Ado About Nothing
As You Like It
Twelfth Night
The Merry Wives of Windsor

RICHARD COURTNEY
Series Editor: Barry Thorne

 SIMON & PIERRE

General Editor: Marian M. Wilson
Series Editor: Barry Thorne
Copy Editor: Jean Paton
Designer: Andy Tong
Printed and Bound in Canada by Metrolitho Inc., Quebec

All quotations from Shakespeare's plays are from the New Penguin edition, except as noted in *End Notes*.Illustrations on pages 170-172 by Richard Courtney.

The writing of this manuscript and the publication of this book were made possible by support from several sources. We would like to acknowledge the generous assistance and ongoing support of the **Canada Council, The Book Publishing Industry Development Program** of the **Department of Canadian Heritage, The Ontario Arts Council**, and **The Ontario Publishing Centre** of the **Ministry of Culture, Tourism and Recreation**.

J. Kirk Howard, President

ISBN 0-88924-230-5
1 2 3 4 5 • 9 7 8 6 5

Canadian Cataloguing in Publication Data

Courtney, Richard

  Shakespeare's world of love

(The Director's Shakespeare series)
Includes bibliographical references.
ISBN 0-88924-230-5

1. Shakespeare, William, 1564-1616 - Comedies.
2. Shakespeare, William, 1564-1616 - Dramatic production. I. Title. II. Series.

PR2981.C68 1994   822.3'3   C94-931157-X

Order from Simon & Pierre Publishing Co. Ltd.

2181 Queen Street East	73 Lime Walk	1823 Maryland Avenue
Suite 301	Headington, Oxford	P.O. Box 1000
Toronto, Canada	England	Niagara Falls, N.Y.
M4E 1E5	0X3 7AD	U.S.A. 14302-1000

We are such stuff
As dreams are made on; and our little life
Is rounded with a sleep.   *(The Tempest,* IV.i.156-158)

for

G. WILSON KNIGHT, C.B.E.
In Memoriam

CONTENTS

Preface   *9*

Introduction   *11*

THE MIDDLE COMEDIES   *21*

MUCH ADO ABOUT NOTHING   *28*

AS YOU LIKE IT   *60*

TWELFTH NIGHT   *98*

THE MERRY WIVES OF WINDSOR   *136*

Conclusion   *162*

   End Notes   *165*

   Works Recommended for Study   *187*

London's most exciting new stage is being built on the south bank of the Thames, where The Shakespeare Globe Trust is recreating Shakespeare's Globe Theatre. Elizabethan building techniques are being used in this authentic recreation.

The Shakespeare Globe Trust is dedicated to the study, appreciation and excellence in performance of Shakespeare's plays and to the faithful reconstruction of his Globe Playhouse near its original London Bankside site, as part of an international, educational and cultural resource centre for people everywhere. Further information is available from: The Shakespeare Globe Trust, Bear Gardens, Bankside, Southwark, London SE1 9EB England.

The photograph shows a model of the theatre and other buildings in the International Shakespeare Globe Centre.

PREFACE

This series of books is intended as an introduction to the plays of William Shakespeare. It is written for stage directors, theatregoers and readers who need to find their way about the plays.

As an actor and director of many of the plays, I have taken a rather different perspective on them: first, that they can only be adequately understood as scripts intended for performance by players; and second, that they focus on the greatest of all themes, the nature of life and death. The first allows us to grasp how the plays *work*. The second demonstrates one reason why Shakespeare's plays are regarded so highly: they address the key issues of our own and every other era by showing that they are universal to humanity in all ages.

The series has a common Introduction and End Notes, which provide basic information for understanding the plays. Acts, scenes, and lines are indicated by round brackets. These divisions into Acts and scenes were added by neo-classical scholars years after Shakespeare's death. But Shakespeare did not intend his plays to be chopped up into small segments. In his time they were played on an unlocalized stage, with one scene flowing into the next.

To recapture this undulation, the plays are examined in the large rhythmical Movements so necessary if they are to be performed. In the theatre, each scene is divided into *beats*, or small rhythmic units; groups of beats with similar emotional effects are *rhythms* (of one or more scenes or within a scene); and groups of these rhythms are *Movements*. In addition, *timing* ranges between fast and slow, and *pace* is the way in which elements of timing are put together.

It is forty years since I first began to direct and act these plays, and almost as long since I began teaching students about them. As a result, I owe much to far more people than I can thank here. But I am under the greatest obligation to the late Professor G. Wilson Knight, for his encouragement and help with my early Shakespearean productions, for the warmth of his personal friendship over several decades, and for his inspiration as an interpreter of Shakespeare. I am grateful to the late Professor Bonamy Dobrée, for his enthusiastic support of my work in directing classic and modern plays; Derek Boughton, for his invaluable support as assistant director in several productions; Philip Stone, the late John Linstrum, Zelda Black, Jacqueline Heywood, Jean Terry Robertson, James Curran, Dorothy Chillingsworth, and other members of experimental drama groups who have worked with me in performances or prepared rehearsals to discover practical ways to overcome specific "knots" in plays; the many players and technical artists, young and old (but particularly the young who continually demonstrate how fresh these plays are), for the long hours we have worked to interpret Shakespeare's plays in the theatre, or in practical interpretation in the classroom. Mention must be made of members of audiences in Britain, Europe, and North America, not just for the warmth of their reactions but specifically for their helpful comments. My thanks also to Sandra M. Burroughs, who typed up the notes for these books; to my wife, Rosemary Courtney, for her usual exemplary editing skills; and to Dr. Barry Thorne, for his expertise.

R. C.
Toronto and
Jackson's Point

INTRODUCTION

READING SHAKESPEARE

The plays of William Shakespeare are among the greatest human achievements. His comedies are funny, his tragedies make us weep, his adventures thrill, amaze and provide us with meaningful experiences. But Shakespeare also means to entertain us.

This does not always happen. Too often, in schools and universities, the plays can be boring, when teachers stop the action to seek out the meaning of a word or discuss the plays like novels. They are *not* novels. We can even be bored in a performance if the actors do not relish Shakespeare, or if they speak his poetry as if it were the telephone directory. The *very last* thing we should be with Shakespeare is bored!

PRINCIPLES

Shakespeare created his plays for *living performance*. They are not "fixed" like a novel, which is the same each time you read it, even if *you* change. One performance of *Hamlet* is never the same as another. Shakespeare wrote his plays for the players who are to act them, for the stage where the people are to come alive, and for the audience who attends them. When we read his plays or see them in a playhouse, they should excite us. We should be carried along with the action, eagerly waiting for the next thrilling moment. If we are bored in the theatre, we are at a bad performance. If we are bored when we read them, we are reading them badly.

There are two complementary ways of reading Shakespeare's plays: as practical working scripts and as works of artistic meaning. Both ways are complementary. If we read them *only* as working scripts for actors, we may misjudge their significance. If we think of them *only* as great poetry with imaginative meanings, we may miss how they work in practice. But if we read them as living entities we combine both methods.

Shakespeare was the leading dramatist of a working professional company: the Lord Chamberlain's Men in Queen Elizabeth I's time, called the King's Men in the reign of James I. Shakespeare was a part-owner of the company. He acted in his own plays and those of others; he may have played the Ghost in *Hamlet*, and he might have "doubled" it with the First Gravedigger. Perhaps. We will never know for certain. But we do know that he was a man of the theatre.

When we read Shakespeare, his play is not simply a story, and we cannot read it as one. We must do what Shakespeare did: we must imagine "in our mind's eye" the events happening, alive and active, performed by actors on an actual stage. We should imagine where they stand, or where they move. If one is to sit on a throne, where will it be? Actors on a stage are *the medium* through which Shakespeare's genius works. As readers, we must focus on the actors and use our imagination, as Ben Jonson said in *The New Inne* (1629):

> I imagine all the world's a play;
> The state, and men's affairs, all passages
> Of life, to spring new scenes, come in, go out,
> And shift, and vanish; and if I have got
> A seat, to sit at ease here, i'mine Inn,
> To see the comedy ...
> Why, will you envy me my happiness?   (I.iii.128-137)

This passage, with its echoes of Shakespeare's more famous:

> All the world's a stage,
> And all the men and women merely players ...
> *(As You Like It*, II.vii.140-141)

tells us that the stage is Shakespeare's world. Even King Lear can lament:

> When we are born we cry that we are come
> To this great stage of fools.   (IV.vi.183-184)

If, as we read, we people the stage with actors in roles, we find out about other human beings: their feelings, their experiences, their manner of living. Then the plays are so engrossing that we can hardly put them down.

But as we study them, more ideas will dawn on us. Perhaps we gain more understanding of the crown, or storms and the sea — always important concepts for Shakespeare. *We must allow our imagination the freedom to understand Shakespeare's artistic* *meanings.* We cannot always put these meanings into words, but as Michael Polanyi says: "We know more than we can tell."* Poetic and symbolic meanings give artistic significance. Putting them into words is the business of criticism. We cannot always use language when we appreciate a play, but we should realize that we are absorbing unconscious meanings.

FINDING PRACTICAL MEANING

When we read a play, we use imagination. Thinking "as if" is imagining. But in order to imagine well, we must understand the basic issues when a dramatist writes for the stage.

RECOGNIZING "THE GAP"

Like other great dramatists who are men of the theatre — and we have such examples as Sophocles, Molière, and Goldoni — Shakespeare wrote plays which have *"a natural gap" between the meaning the words have in themselves and the meaning which the performers give them.* A great playwright knows the skills of actors and the meanings they can convey. In the same way that a composer creates a score, the dramatist writes a play for others to interpret. The words on the page provide one kind of meaning: they are the skeleton for a performance. When the actors speak the text they provide a meaning that gives the skeleton flesh and blood — and life. But the meaning which one actor conveys is not necessarily the same as that of another actor in the same role. They are different people; they have different thoughts, ideas, feelings and emotions. In my production of *The Taming of the Shrew* (Leeds University, 1954), I played Christopher Sly in the Induction; when we took it to Germany the same year, the actor playing Gremio was not available, so I had to double the two parts. This doubling provided a new balance to the ensemble, and people who saw both thought it emphasized different meanings. We must allow for "the gap" as we read Shakespeare's plays, and imagine the play taking place before us.

---

* *Personal Knowledge* (New York: Harper, 1964) 6.

FILLING IN THE MEANING

Then we "fill in" the meanings given to us by the text. We re-create the possibilities of the script within the *play world,* an imagined world in which people (performed by actors) live and breathe. This type of re-creation forms a major contrast with the novel. The printed novel, as we read it, is also a fictional "world," but it is a work of art in itself. The *play world* is not. A great dramatist writes the script so that we can "fill in" the meanings, and only then is it a work of art. We "fill in" the meanings on several levels.

On LEVEL 1 we imagine the events "as if" actors are playing them "here and now," in both space and time. We do so through questions that actors and directors ask. Where does the first scene in *Hamlet* take place? What does it look like? What is the atmosphere? What does each actor do there, moment by moment? Does the atmosphere change during the scene? How do we *feel* "now" in comparison with how we felt a minute ago? *Space and time are the key issues to address in any play.*

These questions lead to LEVEL 2. At this level we reach *questions that are specifically asked by actors,* such as:

- What does Hamlet *think* as he says, "To be or not to be"? "To live" or "not to live" is an important question. Hamlet must be in great personal difficulties to ask himself that. He then asks if it is "nobler" to do one thing rather than another. What does he mean by "nobler"? Actors have to know what people *mean* before they can adequately perform roles.
- Is there a distinction between what the person *thinks* and what he *says?* In some cases there is a difference. When Richard of Gloucester tells his brother Clarence he will help him while he is in the Tower of London, he is lying — he is actually about to arrange for him to be killed.
- Is there a distinction between what the person *consciously thinks* and what he means *unconsciously?* When Olivia asks Viola in *Twelfth Night* what she thinks of her face, or when Claudius tells Hamlet he regards him as a son, what are Olivia's or Claudius' unconscious thoughts?

- What will Hamlet *do* physically when he says, "To be or not to be"? Will he move his arms? Will he stand still or move — and, if he moves, *where* is he moving to, and *why*, and *how*?
- When actors perform together, in pairs or groups, slightly different questions arise. What is Romeo thinking of when Juliet speaks to him from her balcony? How will the nuances of her performance affect Romeo? And how will the players achieve these effects?

On LEVEL 3, *we allow for the "filling in" that specific actors do.* We ask such questions as how would one actor play Romeo in the balcony scene in comparison with another? Or how would different actresses play Juliet in that scene? If the reader has little experience of "live" theatre, then comparisons of performers in film or television might be made — though they perform in a smaller, more intimate way than players on a stage, who act in a grander, larger manner. We might "cast" these performers as the people in the play as we read it.

Finally, we must ask the LEVEL 4 type of question. *What stage objects do the actors use, and how do these objects affect what happens?* Viola in *Twelfth Night* wears the costumes of a woman and of a man. These affect her movement: she can stride about in the male costume, but an Elizabethan bodice and skirt restrict her movements. When Launce enters in *Two Gentlemen of Verona* with his dog, Crab, is it a real dog, or is it imagined (like the rabbit in *Harvey*)? *What is done? Why is it done? And how is it done?* The answers will greatly affect the action of the play. In the Battle of Shrewsbury, Falstaff, a "gross, fat man," is a coward. When I played Falstaff in *1 Henry IV* (Leeds University, 1953; Colne Valley, 1959), I wore armour, a heavy helmet, a sword, a dagger, and heavy padding round my body. During the play I had to fall on the ground and act as if Falstaff were pretending to be dead. Later, I had to carry off the body of Hotspur, a big man also in armour. As an actor, I had to ask in both instances how Falstaff would do it and how it could be done. Such questions illustrate the practical nature of the plays. These questions we do not ask of novels.

FINDING ARTISTIC MEANING

ACTORS OR CHARACTERS?

Too often, critics discuss the plays as if they were dealing *only* with real people and real events, as if they were happening in real life. Yet people and events change with the actors who are playing them. Here we face a major difficulty: *looked at practically, stage roles are actors, but looked at artistically, stage roles are people.* When we read a play we should look at roles in both ways. Unlike novels, plays are simultaneously both practical events and works of art.

Are some dimensions more important than others? This problem was faced by Shakespeare in the late 1590s when the leading comic actor, Will Kempe, left the company and was replaced by Robert Armin. Shakespeare could no longer write the type of part he had created for the quick-witted Kempe, when the role was to be played by the slower Armin. His plays had to be changed. But what happened when the King's Men revived a play in which Kempe had created the role? Armin now had to act it, and the dramatic events changed practically and artistically. A Shakespearean play is always new on stage. With new actors, we in the audience have a different experience from the one we had with other actors.

Readers, like actors and audience, approach the people within a play in two stages: *we go THROUGH the actor to the role, and THROUGH the role to the person.* That is to say, when acting Macbeth about to murder Duncan, the actor asks *what* does Macbeth do? *Why?* And *how?* Will he see a real dagger, or will he imagine it? He has to settle these questions as himself, the actor; as himself in role; and artistically as Macbeth. Similarly in comedy, the actress playing Portia in *The Merchant of Venice* dresses as a male lawyer to defend Antonio in court. At each step in the scene, the actress must ask of Portia *what* she does, *why*, and *how*. The answers to such questions throughout the play make up the total person of Macbeth or Portia.

Readers must also "discover" a text both technically *and* artistically. If you read *The Taming of the Shrew*, you will have to ask the questions I asked when playing Christopher Sly: What does the *actor-in-role* do? (He stays on the chair in which he has been placed.) Why? (Because the Lord is playing a trick on him.) How? (With eyes open as if in a daydream, slurred speech, drunken gestures.) What does the *person* do? (He thinks he dreams.) Why? (He's drunk.) How? (With bewilderment and pleasure.)

POETIC, IMAGINATIVE, AND SYMBOLIC MEANING
Why are Shakespeare's plays so important to humanity? They convey enormous meaning. *King Lear* is not just about an old king who stupidly gives away his kingdom to two of his three daughters, who treat him so badly that he goes mad and dies. That is the broad storyline, which sounds almost like a "soap opera." But there is much more to the play.

First, much of it is in verse. Prose conveys ordinary meaning, but poetry gives us *extra*ordinary meaning. In *King Lear* the old king, turned out of doors by his ungrateful daughters, is caught in a raging storm. If he were going to convey ordinary meaning, he might say:

Listen to that thunder, and that awful wind. It's raining so hard that the churches will get wet, and many chickens and cockerels will drown.

But he does not. What he says is:

Blow, winds, and crack your cheeks! Rage! Blow!
You cataracts and hurricanoes, spout
Till you have drenched the steeples, drowned the cocks!
(III.ii.1-3)

Say that aloud as if you are shouting at the storm (with no pause between "spout" and "Till"). Now that is *not* ordinary! Nor is it "natural"; kings in ancient Britain did not talk like that. Shakespeare takes the language to a new and higher level and gives it richer and more complex meanings.

Poetry helps Shakespeare to expand his imaginative ideas. What Lear says to his daughter, Regan, when she turns against him, is:

You nimble lightnings, dart your blinding flames
Into her scornful eyes! Infect her beauty,
You fen-sucked fogs drawn by the powerful sun,
To fall and blister.   (II.iv.160-163)

Say that, spitting it out in fury and contempt (with no pause between "flames" and "Into"). Now *that* is how to curse! Look at the images Shakespeare uses. "You fen-sucked fogs" has fogs being sucked up from wet fenland by the sun. You can only speak that phrase clearly by emphasizing the "ked" at the end of "sucked" with the "d" as a "t" (thus, "suck't"). Try it once more. Remember the lightning flames blinding Regan's eyes, infecting her beauty and blistering her. It sounds harsh and bitter.

Shakespeare also gives us imaginative meanings: the great storm that buffets Lear is also the storm of life we all must face. It destroys him. How can we stop it from destroying us? His daughters have been warped by the power of kingship, symbolized as a crown. Often to Shakespeare, "crown" signifies temporal power, contrasted with love for others and humanity as a whole. Such ideas extend our thoughts beyond the mere words.

WHAT IS REALISM IN SHAKESPEARE?

The people and the events of a Shakespearean play are *not* "real life." They are dramatic fictions. Yet Shakespeare's works are "life-like," or "true to life." No other dramatist gives us such an accurate picture of human life. But it is a "picture," *not the reality of life itself,* that occurs within the nature and conditions of the stage. This is the kind of experience we try to capture when we read a Shakespearean play. It is grander and more profound than the so-called "reality" of television. Each drama creates a *play world* of its own.

WHAT IS SAID AND DONE

When we read a play by Shakespeare, we create our own reality: we compare the practical with the imaginative. We read the words on the page in two ways, and our comparisons make the script "live" in our minds.

But one particular danger we must notice: *what is said* (the words on the page) does not always easily reveal *what is done.* The reader must treat the script like a detective story: hidden within the text are many clues about *what is done* on the stage. Sometimes the solution is easy, like most stage directions. *Enter Hamlet* is quite simple, except that we must ask *why? Where?* And *how?* But *Exit pursued by a bear* is not as simple as it seems. When we reach the stage implications of the dialogue, sometimes the problem would daunt the most brilliant sleuth. When the old, fat Falstaff is teasing Bardolph about his huge red nose:

BARDOLPH: 'Sblood, I would my face were in your
belly!

FALSTAFF: God-a-mercy! So should I be sure to be
heart-burnt.

Enter Hostess.

FALSTAFF: How now, dame Partlett the hen...

(1 Henry IV, III.iii.48-51)

Why does Falstaff call the Hostess "Dame Partlett the hen," when her name is Mistress Quickly, and there is no other mention of chickens? Is this a hint that her laughter as she enters sounds like a hen's cackle?

When the shrew Katherine is wooed by the brash Petruchio:

KATH: I knew you at the first
You were a movable.

PET: Why, what's a movable?

KATH: A joint-stool.

PET: Thou hast hit it. Come, sit on me.

(The Shrew, II.i.196-198)

What acts does Shakespeare imply here? Much will depend on the players, but Katherine could thrust him away on "movable" so that he sits suddenly on a stool and then pulls her onto his knee with "come sit on me."

As another example, on the battlefield, Lear carries in the dead Cordelia and puts her down:

LEAR: Lend me a looking-glass;
If that her breath will mist or stain the stone,
Why then she lives ...
This feather stirs — she lives!

(King Lear, V.iii.259-263)

To see if a person was still breathing, Elizabethans used mist on a mirror or the movement of a feather. Even if someone finds a mirror for Lear on a battlefield, where does the feather come from? Probably from nowhere. The others know Cordelia is dead and give Lear nothing. In his distress, Lear imagines both mirror and feather.

KINDS OF REALITY

Shakespeare knew two kinds of reality. One was the reality of Renaissance England in which apprentices, burghers, and aristocrats were an audience watching a play. They lived in a world of ordinary experience: the *actual world*. Reality was what everyone with common sense knew it to be, and those who did not were dreaming or were "mad."

But within that ordinary, commonsense reality was another: the *play world*. Similar to the "world" of the child at play, which children believe to be as "real" as the everyday, the *play world* on a stage that Shakespeare's audience knew was not actual, not "real" as the world they lived in was real. But a play performed on a stage might *appear* to be real. Then the actors were not actors but flesh and blood persons who laughed and cried like people in the actual world. The reality of the *play world* was imaginative: created in the mind of the playwright, the actors, and the audience together. When Jaques in *As You Like It* says, "All the world's a stage," Shakespeare compares the two realities in a double metaphor: life is like a theatre, and theatre is like life. And this is the metaphor Shakespeare uses throughout his plays.

But the Renaissance audience was not *quite* sure of the difference. They did not, for example, clearly separate the actual (the natural) from the *super*natural, nor the supernatural from the dream. Thus at the end of his life, Shakespeare creates for Prospero the lines:

> We are such stuff
> As dreams are made on ...   *(The Tempest*, IV.i.156-157)

Here, it is not that life is like theatre, or that theatre is like life, but that life *is* a play, and that people are created from such dreams.

The complication comes when we, today, are part of an audience for one of Shakespeare's plays. If there were two realities in Shakespeare's time, the ordinary Renaissance actuality and the *play world* of, say, *Hamlet* on the stage, are we in a modern audience, then, another reality? And what reality does the reader have?

You, the reader, must answer that for yourself ...

THE MIDDLE COMEDIES

LOVE & COMEDY

hakespeare's Middle Comedy consists of four major plays: three superb romantic comedies in *Much Ado About Nothing, As You Like It,* and *Twelfth Night,* and an uproarious farcical comedy, *The Merry Wives of Windsor.* All were written just before 1600, and all are immensely popular in performance, with each age providing its own distinguished productions. All make superb theatre.

The four are comedies of love. The first three are among the greatest comedies in any language; with them Shakespeare reaches his peak as a creator of romantic comedy. *Much Ado About Nothing, As You Like It,* and *Twelfth Night* have much in common. They are filled with pleasurable joy from beginning to end — even *Much Ado,* which has its dark moments when villainy for a time threatens to win. Like Shakespeare's earlier comedies, they focus on the psychology of lovers; but now they include some of Shakespeare's greatest comic roles: Beatrice and Benedick, Rosalind, and Viola with Orsino and Olivia. Part of the reason for the plays' theatrical success is that they include very different people living in diverse atmospheres. The plays occur in specific mental spaces: the Messina of *Much Ado* is Italianate with a dark touch that leads to *Measure for Measure;* in *As You Like It* the Forest of Arden is quintessentially English with the hints of ancient rituals in the greenwood; and in *Twelfth Night* the glory that is Illyria exists nowhere but in the imagination, as it casts its spell over the people who live there. These factors affect not only the actors and their style of playing, and the nature of the stage design, but also the reading of the plays. We must know where the people are in order to assess what they do and how they do it.

In these plays of love we should note the power of the women: Beatrice, Rosalind, and Viola. Given the gender attitudes of Elizabethans, Shakespeare makes a very powerful and unusual case for female power. Benedick is the only male lover who has the depth and strength of these remarkable young women. In the earlier comedies, only Portia is as rich a personality as the men. But at the end of *Much Ado,* Beatrice appears to share power with Benedick, although we suspect that this brilliant woman will control their marriage. Rosalind is the focus of *As You Like It;* remarkably, she is the female controlling agent of the plot set within a male world. At the end she freely, and of her own choice, gives her power away to the patriarchal society — largely, we suspect, because Shakespeare bows to the conventions of his time. Viola is the focus of *Twelfth Night,* but she does not control the plot like Rosalind; her disguise does. The other active agents are romantic delusion (Orsino and Olivia), romantic realism (Viola and Sebastian), and chaos (Sir Toby and Maria). What makes Viola so remarkable is the delight we take in her as a person, and her extreme facility in adapting to all and every circumstance.

We speak of Shakespeare's "comic world" as being different from, say, that of Molière or Goldoni, Sheridan or Shaw. Shakespeare's "comic world" combines three themes: love, role-playing, and the idea of losing oneself to find oneself — essentially a religious concept which Shakespeare interprets comically. All of his comedies use these themes, but Shakespeare varies their interplay in two main ways: their relative emphasis in the design of the play and the degree of implicit or explicit reference.

But, with few exceptions, *each of Shakespeare's comedies occurs in its own very special "world."* Each has a rich, highly distinctive, and coherent mental and physical space that is defined by role playing. In each play, the world is consistent and is shared by its inhabitants, however unlike each other they are as people. The comedies discussed here rely heavily on deception and disguise, not simply as forms of theatricality (which can be the case in the earlier comedies) but as important elements of theme, structure, texture, and the unique atmosphere of each play.

Within each "world," Shakespeare uses *a double spatial structure*, of which there are two kinds: those that move between two locations *(As You Like It)*; and those which are set in a single location but move between two internal spaces *(Much Ado* and *Twelfth Night)*. In each case, the created worlds are fully coherent and focus upon love.

Shakespeare's comic coherence begins with *The Shrew,* but it does not become truly distinctive until *The Dream.* Role playing is used to create broad spatial contrasts, such as those that distinguish Athens from fairyland. In many plays, there is a contrast of two locations: Belmont and Venice in *The Merchant;* the Forest of Arden and Duke Frederick's court in *As You Like It.* Venice can be judged by Belmont, and Belmont by Venice, Arden by the court and vice versa. Shakespeare achieves this expansion of spatial contexts by contrasting two inner "worlds" and the role-playing within them.

Contrast is also used in those plays that have only one physical world. Within a single locality, Shakespeare can make use of two interior worlds and play one off against another. These two worlds can be two levels of society; then each throws light on the qualities and shortcomings of the other, as they do in *Love's Labour's Lost.* In *Much Ado,* we have the interaction of two social worlds in the way the thick-witted Dogberry and Verges bring to light the truth about Hero, a truth which the people of high society are incapable of discovering.

In *Twelfth Night* there is the rich parallel of Orsino and Olivia who choose (mistakenly) to play the roles of lovers, as compared to Viola who changes from a female to a male role while remaining true to herself. Despite the fact that Viola and Sebastian have been shipwrecked (i.e., they have come from somewhere else), Illyria is the entire spatial context for *Twelfth Night,* and a splendidly romantic place it is, populated by some of the most wonderful people of Shakespeare's genius: the vital Viola, the idealistic Duke, the beautiful Olivia, the haughty Malvolio, the reprobate Sir Toby, the timid Sir Andrew, the resourceful Maria, the brilliant fool Feste, and the practical Fabian. One cannot find these people anywhere but in Illyria.

In *Much Ado,* Shakespeare shows the complex happenings

that result when Don Pedro, Don John, Claudio and Benedick come from the wars to the house of Leonato in Messina, where Hero and Beatrice wait for their husbands-to-be. In *Twelfth Night* and *Much Ado*, the locality is single, and, within it, the action is the working out of the relationships between people. Shakespeare brings two groups (the "insiders" and the "outsiders") together in one locality, and the play emerges from the interaction of their roles.

There is a continuous change in Shakespeare's attitude to role playing, which is evident in comparing his early comedies with *Much Ado*, *As You Like It*, *Twelfth Night* and then those that follow. All his comedies imply that there is an ideal role that suits each character perfectly, and he or she has the potential to fulfil it successfully. In *The Shrew*, such a role is said to be "aptly fitted" and "naturally performed." If so acted, it provides personal well-being for the individual and stability for society. In *The Shrew* and all his early comedies, Shakespeare is optimistic that people can realize the ideal and that they can do so through human effort alone (e.g., Katherine). But as the comedies follow on one another, Shakespeare becomes less optimistic. In *As You Like It*, Jaques is weary about all the world being a stage. In *Twelfth Night*, Viola's role-change eventually brings her happiness, but not without heartache in her conversations with Orsino. And in *Much Ado*, things are much darker: the glittering dialogue of the roles taken by Beatrice and Benedick is seen to cover matters of life and death, when Beatrice suddenly says: "Kill Claudio!" In *Much Ado* roles focus on the love vs. hate (true vs. false) masks of Beatrice and Benedick. Later, once tragedy becomes Shakespeare's primary mode, there is a more radical change. Even in comedies like *Measure for Measure* and *All's Well*, Shakespeare's attitude to role playing is pessimistic, and the comedy is tempered with a tragic tone.

It is *Much Ado* that leads us to Shakespeare's later "problem plays." In structure, at least, the three comedies comprise a coherent group. But they also have a great range in mood: from *As You Like It* at one extreme to *All's Well* and *Measure for Measure* at the other. The villains of the middle comedies — the usurping Duke and Oliver of *As You Like It*, and Don John of *Much Ado* — are conventional types whose schemes simply help to move the action onwards. But *Much Ado* also contains the morally ambiguous Don Pedro: what he eventually achieves is pleasing, even if he is not. He is less a genuine villain than a comic manipulator, like many others. But unlike him, these "directors" are attractive people: Petruchio, Portia, the Friar of *Much Ado*, the Merry Wives, and Rosalind. *Much Ado* begins an increasingly darkening mood in Shakespeare's comedy. In *Much Ado* most of the playlets are not just the result of villainy (as are those of Don John) or temporary delusion (like Claudio's performance in the church). Rather, they include the idea that, with a little help, the victim of the playlet will improve, and both he and the others will be in a happier state. This may, of course, be the result of Ben Jonson's influence. In *All's Well*, however, the playlets are even more serious.

In his early plays, Shakespeare used another new structure for comedy, based on the idea of a journey. This kind of comedy was entirely new to plays and had no precedent, classical or otherwise. It depends on a change of locality, on the adventures of one or more people on a journey from one place to another. This comic form began in the Hellenistic romance, upon which were built the sixteenth century narratives that Shakespeare knew and used as sources for many comedies. He translated this narrative form into dramatic structures. He began with *The Two Gentlemen of Verona*, and he returned to the form regularly. Here, in his three great comedies of love, he adapts the structure to bring about the main action of the plays. In *As You Like It*, a whole group of people travels from the court to the forest and, at the end, returns; in *Twelfth Night* there is the arrival of strangers; and in *Much Ado* the victorious Don Pedro and his defeated half-brother Don John return to Messina. In later plays, Shakespeare returns more directly to the journey: *All's Well* shows Helena at Rousillon, at Paris, in Italy, and again at Rousillon, always in quest of Bertram; and several of the last plays are based on journeys.

The mockery in the three great romantic comedies is usually gentle. They are concerned not with the unpleasantness of life but with the joys of the human experience. Nor is *As You Like It* a play with a great deal of uproarious laughter in it; rather, it is an excellent example of the kind of comedy that Sir Philip Sidney talked of in his *Apology for Poetry* (c. 1580) as based on "delight," in contrast to comedy focused on laughter, like *The Merry Wives*. It has been said that delight has a joy in it, but laughter has only a scornful tickling. There is little "scornful tickling" in *As You Like It* or *Twelfth Night*, unless Malvolio is over-played, and we start to feel sorry for him. In these plays, if the characters fall into absurdity we laugh *at* them. But mostly we laugh *with* them, enjoying the way they face the trials of love and life and overcome them. The "scornful tickling" in *Much Ado* centers on the wonderful Dogberry, probably the last character that the great clown Will Kempe created for Shakespeare.

These three great romantic comic plays return comedy to its origins: the celebration of a festival. In the ancient Near East, it was "the sacred marriage" ritual that celebrated the renewal of the cosmos, the earth, and humanity. Theatre, like ritual, has always centred on human existence — on "life, copulation, and death." *As You Like It* is the most ritualistic of the three, with echoes of the most ancient rites. In all three we rejoice in the human situation, we celebrate that human difficulties are overcome, and union is achieved in the marriage ritual that almost always ends a comedy.

The fourth play of Shakespeare's Middle Comedy is *The Merry Wives of Windsor*. Here we mostly laugh *at*, not *with*, people. And "scornful tickling" is everywhere. It is majestically farcical and, with *The Shrew*, is Shakespeare's most significant contribution to this theatrical genre. But, like *The Shrew*, it has been mishandled by critics who often regard farce as a lesser form than, say, comedy. This is due to the fact that they have largely treated plays as literature only. They have ignored the fact that farce is predominantly theatrical. Reading a farce takes a great deal of imagination because its essence cannot be captured in print. For example, how do you write down the fun involved when a pompous person is hit with a custard pie?

The *Merry Wives* has always been one of Shakespeare's most popular plays with audiences. His main farces, *The Comedy of Errors*, *The Shrew*, and *The Merry Wives*, lack subtlety (as farces should), but each commences from the idea that the leading people are surprised: they find themselves in unexpected places and situations. In *The Merry Wives*, Shakespeare takes Falstaff and his companions away from their association with Prince Hal and the Boar's Head; then he imagines them in a totally different world, that of the citizens of Windsor. The play is said to show Sir John in love; but it actually describes his penury and his lust. The core of the play is that Falstaff shows his essential self (his lechery and his belief in his natural gifts), but he is confronted by the citizens with their more formidable advantages. The play tells of his inevitable defeats, and the audience enjoys every moment.

Finally we should note that this superb farce, and the three equally great romantic comedies, were written in Shakespeare's most prolific period. Alongside them, and within the same short period of time, he also wrote *Henry IV (Parts 1 and 2)*, *Henry V*, *Julius Caesar*, and *Hamlet*. It is little wonder that we are amazed at his genius. All of these masterpieces, probably written in about four years, still enthral audiences all over the world.

MUCH ADO ABOUT NOTHING

ABOUT NOTHING

uch Ado About Nothing is a brilliant play, one of Shakespeare's best. Performing it, the players make a major discovery: it is difficult to say what *kind* of play it is. It is primarily a love comedy, of course, and it is a splendid play to read as well as a thrilling piece to attend in the theatre. But what *kind* of love comedy is it?

Much Ado is Shakespeare's nearest play to a comedy of manners. The main theme is Pride (*hubris*) and its influence on convention or "fashion": what is "proper" to do, or not to do, in a society; and, above all, what it is fashionable to be *seen* to do, or *seen* not to do. Pride motivates most people in the play, particularly Claudio, Don Pedro, Leonato — and Dogberry, one of Shakespeare's greatest clowns. But although *Much Ado* is somewhat like a comedy of manners, it is like no other.

Much Ado is also Shakespeare's nearest play to a satiric comedy. It satirizes the fashionable attitudes of the time, both of individuals and of society as a whole. But it is not like other satiric comedies of Shakespeare's time; for example, it is not so acerbic as those of his colleague, rival, and friend, Ben Jonson. Shakespeare cuts through appearance, but without Jonson's acidity. When we perform *Much Ado* and Jonson's *Volpone* in the theatre, the players discover a major difference: Jonson requires a sharp intellect and cynical eye, but Shakespeare needs a more human touch. Nor is *Much Ado*'s bite as sharp as Molière's *Tartuffe* or *The Miser,* nor as brutal as Wycherley's *The Country Wife,* nor as sleazy as Vanbrugh's *The Relapse.* It is thus difficult to say that Shakespeare's play is a fully satiric comedy.

Much Ado is a genuine comedy which theatre audiences relish, but a lot of it is not amusing at all. It raises serious questions about the human condition: in our relations with others, what do we "know"? What is the difference between true wit (Beatrice and Benedick) and false wit or pretentious wisdom (Claudio)? How significant is the concept of feminine honour (Hero) in a society? What is love, and what is "love's truth"? What is the relation of love between two people, and love in the Neoplatonic and Christian sense — specifically in Hero's redemptive sacrifice, her feigned death, and "return to life"? None of these questions is fully answered in *Much Ado*. Shakespeare, after all, creates a play, not a philosophic thesis. But the people on the stage must deal with these questions while we in the audience struggle with them on their behalf. And both actors and audience must face some nasty surprises, in life as in theatre, such as when, in the middle of a witty love dialogue, Beatrice suddenly turns to Benedick and demands, "Kill Claudio" — one of the greatest moments in all comic theatre.

The title tells us the sort of play it is. It is *about* nothing, that is, pride, or false appearances, and *with* nothing, that is: stereotypes about people on insufficient evidence, hearsay or gossip. Elizabethans pronounced "nothing" as "noting," and understood other meanings: the musical "notes" of harmony, the essence of marriage; and the way people "notice" things, as Claudio notes that a lady at Hero's window is courting a stranger and assumes the worst. By giving the play the title of *Much Ado About Nothing*, Shakespeare tells us much. But he also demonstrates that labelling plays like "comedy of manners" or "satiric comedy" is very misleading. Like all of Shakespeare's plays, it is unique. But, perhaps, *Much Ado* is more unique than others.

THE COMIC WORLD

Each of Shakespeare's comedies has its own comic world. Some things all his comedies share, but each is distinctively different from the others. In *Much Ado* there are clear social levels — upper, middle, and lower class — just like Shakespeare's audience. The play appealed to everyone. Only the aristocrats knew that when Beatrice talks about marriage in terms of dancing (II.i) she is parodying *Orchestra, A Poem for Dancing,* by Sir John Davies. The middle-class shopkeepers identified with Leonato, a father sorely tried by his daughter. The groundlings adored the spectacle, the dancing, the great clown Dogberry who can do nothing right and, even funnier, the *terribly* serious Don Pedro. And the absurd Deformed would have brought the house down.

Perhaps the essence of *Much Ado* is best captured by Beatrice after Don Pedro has praised her wit:

PED: Your silence most offends me, and to be merry
           best becomes you; for out o'question you were
           born in a merry hour.
BEA: No, sure, my lord, my mother cried; but then
           there was a star danced, and under that was I
           born.   (II.i.306-310)

Beatrice and Benedick are the wittiest couple in all drama, and the wit of the whole is satirical, but *Much Ado* celebrates human goodness, like all Shakespeare's comedies. The high spirits of Beatrice and Benedick, with the low spirits of Dogberry, remain with us after we leave the theatre. Shakespeare calculates his remarkable effects with characteristic shrewdness.

This world is a fiction, needless to say, but it has an extraordinary likeness to life. It is decidedly not *real* life; it is a *theatrical* life that operates in a similar way. All the main people live in one house; they eavesdrop on each other, crack jokes or tease one another, or go off to a meal or a dance (facts vital to the stage designer). They may talk a heightened form of language, but it is conversational, even colloquial. And their informality gives their actions the *appearance* of spontaneity. It is one side of Shakespeare's genius that he provides us with a world that is like life, yet we always know it is played by actors in a theatre. Thus he raises another important question: what is life and what is illusion?

The specific comic world of *Much Ado* has a particular quality: all the characters have their personal pride: they believe their personal individualities (egos), right or wrong. These beliefs are a major target for Shakespeare's critique of his own society. The key to his satire lies in Dogberry, who is "Everyman" in the role of the Constable. Any society that can tolerate him in this role must fully support the personal ego. Consider his views on how to handle delinquents. According to Verges, Dogberry has "been always called a merciful man." "Truly," Dogberry agrees, "I would not hang a dog by my will, much more a man who hath any honesty in him." His relaxed ideas of enforcing the law, while they may resemble the wise forbearance recommended and practised by Friar Francis, are not due to kindness or moral indifference. Take thieves, for example. Says Dogberry, "the less you meddle or make with them, why, the more is for your honesty," and he has scriptural authority for his view: "they that touch pitch will be defiled" (III.iii.51-62).

Defiling is vital to the plot. The danger of contamination to the personal ego runs through the play. Claudio and the others shrink from Hero because they fear contamination. This makes them accessories to that master thief, Deformed. Also, as Hero discovers to her cost, once their pride is hurt they want to scourge moral evil with increased enthusiasm — a Shakespearean touch that is true in all ages, including our own. Dogberry has a similar enthusiasm when, subsequently, he uses the full severity of the law against the "naughty varlet" who has called him ass. In this fictional Messina, the strong individualist fears not the law.

Part of the comic world of *Much Ado* is a new attitude to relations between the sexes. Beatrice and Benedick have cast off the restraints of the courtly tradition of romantic love (so brilliantly shown in *As You Like It*) for a newer freedom. They represent an emergent outlook on life that was beginning in the late 1590s. Both presume they are immune to loving the other — much to our amusement — but when they do find love, they really value it. Then there is no pretence between them. On the stage, this transition between one tradition and another is very difficult to bring off, and requires considerable acting skill. My approach to the problem (Leeds Arts Theatre Experimental Group, 1952) was to rehearse the players alternately in the two traditions. Once they understood the two styles of performance, they were able to successfully put them together.

HISTORY OF THE PLAY

Much Ado was probably written between 1597 and 1600. It was not listed in Francis Meres' list of 1598, which does include a Shakespearean play called *Love's Labour's Won,* which may be *Much Ado* under another name. The Folio text (1623) of *Much Ado* was printed from the only earlier text, the 1600 Quarto. This occasionally assigns speeches to "Kempe" instead of Dogberry so, as we know that the actor Will Kempe, the famous clown who created the role, left the Lord Chamberlain's Men late in 1599, the play can probably be dated 1598-1599.

The Beatrice and Benedick story, together with Dogberry and the Watch, is mostly Shakespeare's invention. The Hero-Claudio plot, of Roman origin and known in Italy during the Renaissance, had a number of English versions before Shakespeare's play. These included Spenser's *The Faerie Queene* (1590) and a translation of Ariosto's *Orlando Furioso* (1591).

Will Kempe was probably the greatest Dogberry. The play was enjoyed in Shakespeare's time, but during the Restoration it was mingled with *Measure for Measure* by William d'Avenant into the hybrid *The Law Against Lovers* (1662). Other versions followed. By the end of the eighteenth century, however, Shakespeare's own *Much Ado* was again a favourite play of the public, and so it has remained. Sir Henry Irving directed a great production of *Much Ado* at the Lyceum Theatre (1882), in which he and Ellen Terry disagreed about the interpretation of the "Kill Claudio" scene. John Gielgud was a brilliantly spoken and lofty Benedick with two superb Beatrices: the sincere Peggy Ashcroft (1950) and the brilliant Diana Wynyard (1951). It was fascinating to see how the play changed between the two performances.* Today *Much Ado* remains one of Shakespeare's most popular plays.

---

* For theatre history see Salgado (1975), Sprague (1944, 1953) and Sprague and Trewin (1970).

STRUCTURE AND PLOT

In a typical Shakespearean "double structure," there are two plots and some low comedy. The main plot of *Much Ado*, derived from Ariosto, is not particularly comic but is quite melodramatic. It has Benedick's friend Claudio deceived into believing that Hero, Beatrice's cousin, has a lover before their wedding. He denounces her, and she faints as if dead. The play is loved mainly for its subplot: there is a fiery mutual attraction between a confirmed spinster and a confirmed bachelor — Beatrice and Benedick — whose duel of words, sexual and very witty, is the most popular part of the play. The friends of Beatrice and Benedick allow them to hear, separately, that each is in love with the other, and the contrivance works. Claudio suffers remorse, Hero recovers, and the two pairs dance into marriage. The low comedy is provided by the members of the Night Watch, who by chance clear Hero of Claudio's accusation. They are led by the self-important Dogberry, a richly funny character loved by all audiences. He murders the language ("Comparisons are odorous") in an inversion of the word play of Beatrice and Benedick. Deceit and disguise abound: Beatrice and Benedick initially hide their feelings from one another; and victimizers in one case of deception (Hero, Claudio and friends) are victims in another. No crowd of people in a Shakespearean world more likes to play "the game," to exchange the roles of deceiver and deceived.

Much Ado has its own natural rhythms which create four sequential Movements:
- The long Exposition prepares for the Hero-Claudio marriage; Don John plots and schemes (I.i-II.i).
- Mainly about the Beatrice-Benedick story, the Movement ends with Claudio's denunciation of Hero (II.ii-IV.i).
- Vengeance is sought for wounded honour (IV.ii-V.iii).
- Hero is resurrected and all is unified (V.iv).

This structure is very different from *As You Like It*, where virtually all the action takes place in Act I, and then there is nothing until the finale. In *Much Ado*, the main plot and sub-plot do not get under way until the second act is nearly over. At the start, Shakespeare presents some contests that quickly establish the devices of deception, eavesdropping, fashion, and fighting. There is little action to begin with, but as the play addresses gossip among a large group of people, there is a great deal of movement and a comic pace that keeps the audience's interest.

As a result of this unique structure, the director of *Much Ado* should take great care in the First Movement, particularly the opening scene. Here there are lines which, on stage, require "pointing" (or stressing), because they tell what has happened or foreshadow what is to come. Stage "pointing" indicates which words and phrases must be emphasized and which need not. For example, the word "fashion" runs through the play as a whole. "Good Signor Leonato," Don Pedro tells his host, "The fashion of the world is to avoid cost, and you encounter it" (I.i.89-91). It is a conventionally courteous remark, but the first clause gives us a truth which becomes increasingly apparent as the play continues. The second clause is ironic considering Leonato's later action. He willingly incurs expense for hospitality, particularly when his guest is a distinguished nobleman; yet he cannot spend any kindness when he thinks that his daughter, Hero, has destroyed some of his self-esteem.

THE ACTION

In the theatre, *Much Ado* is formed around five scenes using large groups of people in beautiful costumes: the arrival of Don Pedro's retinue (I.i), the masked ball (II.i), the two church scenes (IV.i and V.iii), and the finale and dance (V.iv). These are intended to be eye-catching with group movements of most of the company. As Don Pedro and his men have just returned from war, their arrival might include banners. The masked ball is the most spectacular, with conversation taking place between dances, and while the dances continue.

The First Movement: Exposition

Don Pedro, Prince of Arragon, arrives in Messina, with his illegitimate brother, Don John, and two young Italian noblemen, his friends Claudio and Benedick. Don Pedro has recently defeated his brother in battle. Now reconciled,

they visit Leonato before returning home. Claudio falls in
love with Leonato's daughter, Hero. Beatrice and Benedick
banter. Don Pedro says he will act as proxy on behalf of
Claudio for Hero's hand (I.i).

The play opens just before the arrival at Leonato's house of
Don Pedro and his retinue. The audience is prepared for
Claudio as the hero because he has been brave in battle (he
performed "feats of a lion"). Claudio tells Don Pedro that
falling in love with Hero has changed him utterly:

> O, my lord,
> When you went onward on this ended action,
> I looked upon her with a soldier's eye,
> That liked, but had a rougher task in hand
> Than to drive liking to the name of love;
> But now I am returned and that war-thoughts
> Have left their places vacant, in their rooms
> Come thronging soft and delicate desires,
> All prompting me how fair young Hero is,
> Saying I liked her ere I went to wars.   (275-284)

This passage tells us much about Elizabethan psychology
[see *End Notes*]. Claudio says that the "soft and delicate desires"
which led him to love Hero poured into his consciousness as if
filling an empty jar; his prior "war-thoughts" had already dissi-
pated, leaving "vacant" places ready to be filled. This "conceit"
pictures Claudio as being an empty vessel without identity or
personality until he is filled with his new role as a lover. Only in
the tragedies does Shakespeare normally focus on moments of
complete emptiness, of complete absence of "character." Here,
the passive way in which Claudio takes the role of lover is consistent with his inability, throughout most of the play, to play a
part effectively. Indeed, Claudio bungles his role as a lover.

We are also well prepared for Benedick as someone who
mocks, and whose antagonism to women may quickly turn to
love. There are hints throughout the play that Beatrice (Hero's
cousin) and Benedick have met before and might even have
had a previous affair. But Shakespeare tells us no more than
this. Benedick and Beatrice "never meet but there's a skirmish
of wit between them" (lines 58-59).

This scene, like the play as a whole, is full of word play,
although it is not as extreme as in *Love's Labour's Lost.* There

are notorious puns: e.g., "he'll be meet with you," when *meet* implies "proper," "encounter," and "meat" (which can also imply "man's flesh"); "He is no less than a stuffed man," when *stuffed* implies "full of food," "full of useless learning," and "pregnant"; and, "He is a very valiant trencherman," when *trencherman* implies "soldier," "diner," and "sexual partner." As in many Shakespeare plays, some puns are thought vulgar by delicate moderns, but in his time they would have been thought amusing; Elizabethans were very natural about bodily functions. The play is full of wise sayings and proverbs and various styles of imagery based on high society, animals, sickness, crime, and religion (Benedick will "die at the stake" to defy love).

Don Pedro tells Claudio that he will act as his proxy for Hero's hand. They are overheard by at least two people: Antonio's servant and Borachio. As *Much Ado* is a comedy, overhearing is an occasion for stage "business": Don Pedro and Claudio try to talk secretly; the others try to eavesdrop.

> *A servant of Leonato's brother, Antonio, has overheard Don Pedro and Claudio talking of Hero but has mistakenly reported that Don Pedro will woo her for himself. Leonato intends to tell Hero of this (I.ii).*

When Leonato hears that Don Pedro is to woo his daughter, he says, "we will hold it as a dream, till it appear itself" (line 18). The idea of dream is, thus, united to the theme of illusion and reality [see *End Notes*].

This scene introduces Antonio, Leonato's brother, who later challenges Claudio. He and his brother are the two "old men" of the plot: Leonato is fussy, Antonio is suspicious and a gossip. Their age becomes significant in V.i, when "the old men" confront "the young men."

> *Don John and his servant, Conrade, are informed by another servant, Borachio, of what he, too, has overheard. Don John decides to think up some mischief (I.iii).*

Don John is the arch-villain of the piece, but, as *Much Ado* is a comedy, he is a cardboard villain. He is deadly serious, melancholy, evil by nature, and contemptuous of human feelings. He is quite open about his villainy — indeed, he tells us more about it than he shows us. He wants to destroy the marriage, because he is envious of Claudio. Shakespeare images Don John as both an animal and a bird:

> ... I am a plain-dealing villain. I am trusted with a muzzle and enfranchised with a clog [a beast of burden]; therefore I have decreed not to sing in my cage. If I had my mouth, I would bite; if I had my liberty, I would do my liking. In the meantime, let me be that I am, and seek not to alter me. (29-34)

Conrade and Borachio are convincing supporting villains. Borachio (whose name may indicate that he drinks) was born a gentleman. The three of them, as comic but deadly serious villains, are often directed as a stylized trio on the modern stage.

> *Leonato's masked ball. Don John tells Claudio (as if he were Benedick) that Don Pedro intends to marry Hero himself. Claudio tells Benedick, who tells Don Pedro. He tells Benedick that Beatrice is furious: a masked dancer (it was Benedick) told her Benedick's views of her. Don Pedro tells Claudio he has won Hero for him. Before the wedding, they will trick Beatrice and Benedick into falling in love with each other (II.i).*

This is a spectacular scene with music and everyone dancing in masks and colourful costumes, some better than others: Antonio is literally palsied with age (line 102). There are mistakes of identity. Many modern directors use the ongoing dance so that existing dancers come forward as they act their playlets, and use the masks to emphasize the themes of mistaken identity and appearance and reality.

The (false) idea that Hero is actually wooed by Don Pedro and Benedick's return to Messina lead Beatrice into hilarious and witty dialogue; the cruelty of her remarks to Benedick indicates that she is under some strain. She uses religious imagery about men: they are wicked and unredeemed, and so need grace and purification. But she has her eye on Benedick: "I am sure he is in the fleet; I would he had boarded me" (line 128). Benedick's antipathy to Beatrice is complete. Here Benedick is playing four main roles: as an outsider, he is a critic of society; as an enemy but potential lover of Beatrice, he reacts to her personality; as a soldier, he thinks about emotions in terms of strategy and describes Beatrice's words as "poniards"; and as a messenger, he is a deceiver without knowing it.

Don John's plot almost works: Claudio falls for the trick. "The Prince woos for himself" (line 159), he bitterly reflects, and his suspicion is reinforced moments later when the real Benedick tells him, "the Prince hath got your Hero ... But did you think the Prince would have served you thus?" (lines 176-180). With Don Pedro's assurances, Claudio returns to high spirits. Hero is a clone to Claudio: she is equally passive, obedient to her father, and stereotypical in her reactions to Claudio.

Don Pedro, having tested his wings, is ready for more ambitious "practice." Aspiring to the role of Cupid, he sees a possible match between Beatrice and Benedick and plots to "fashion it" (line 341). Both are outspoken advocates of the single life, and Don Pedro undertakes to bring the two warriors "into a mountain of affection, th'one with th'other" (lines 339-340) and make each believe the other has secretly succumbed to love.

The Second Movement: Intrigue and Reversal

> Borachio tells Don John that Margaret, Hero's servant, will be at Hero's window at night: it will appear she is Hero in love with Borachio. Don John will tell Don Pedro and Claudio that Hero is a wanton and bring them on cue (II.ii).

Borachio shrewdly suggests that he and Margaret can be mistaken for Hero and another lover in the darkness, so that Hero can appear to be an "approved wanton," fit to be scorned and cast away. Don John, in his role as dutiful informer, should "intend a kind of zeal both to the Prince and Claudio" and lead them to spy on the scene.

> Don Pedro, Leonato, Hero, and Claudio talk of Beatrice being in love with Benedick so that he can overhear them. Benedick decides to take pity on her and return her love (II.iii).

While Don John's plot nears its climax, another conspiracy is being hatched. After Balthazar has sung, "Sigh no more, ladies," Don Pedro, conspiring with Claudio and Leonato, arranges for Benedick in the arbour to overhear a fictional conversation to the effect that Beatrice secretly languishes for him. They begin:

DON P: Come hither, Leonato. What was it you told me of today, that your niece Beatrice was in love with Signor Benedick?

CLAUD: *[Aside]* O, aye; stalk on, stalk on, the fowl sits. — I did never think that lady would have loved any man.

LEON: No, nor I neither; but most wonderful that she should dote so on Signor Benedick; whom she hath in all outward behaviours seemed ever to abhor.

BENE: *[Aside]* Is't possible? Sits the wind in that corner?   (91-100)

The scene is delicious, and Benedick emerges from hiding completely convinced. He thinks of Beatrice in his own terms and determines that her love "must be requited," even though he will be the subject of jests as he said he would never fall in love. He exits in search of her picture.

Hero designs it so that she and her two gentlewomen talk of Benedick's love for Beatrice in such a way that Beatrice overhears them. Beatrice vows to return his love (III.i).

Almost immediately thereafter, Hero and her two attendants, Margaret and Ursula, play the identical trick on Beatrice in the arbour (except that they speak in verse). Hero reveals a sense of humour that is delightful as she arranges for Beatrice to overhear that Benedick is pining for her:

HERO: No, truly, Ursula, she is too disdainful;
         I know her spirits are as coy and wild
         As haggards of the rock.

URS: But are you sure
         That Benedick loves Beatrice so entirely?
                                               (34-37)

Apart from attacking Beatrice's pride and scorn, Hero also reveals the thievery of "fashion": the spoils are most frequently the qualities which, in the Shakespearean sense, are "natural": that is, those which nurture and solidify basic interpersonal bonds. Earlier, Beatrice said this fault applied to Benedick who wears his faith, "but as the fashion of his hat; it ever changes with the next block" (I.i.69-71). Now Hero shrewdly explains that Beatrice cannot love because

> her wit
> Values itself so highly that to her
> All matter else seems weak. (52-54)

Beatrice emerges from hiding overwhelmed, bidding contempt and maiden pride farewell. Unlike Benedick's huffing and puffing in the parallel scene, she goes into a flight of passion which, because it is in verse, seems more artificial than Benedick's response. She vows to return Benedick's love.

> *Don Pedro, Claudio, and Leonato tease Benedick and*
> *accuse him of being in love. Don John tells Don Pedro and*
> *Claudio that Hero is false, and arranges with them to*
> *observe her at her window that night (III.ii).*

Don John takes Borachio's hint (in II.ii) to warn Claudio that it would "better fit" his honour to put sentiment aside and break off his intended marriage. The mere suggestion (without any evidence whatsoever) of damage to his self-esteem makes Claudio resolve to shame the unsuspecting Hero at the altar. This aim is immediately accepted by Don Pedro. The overriding pride and self-esteem of Claudio, Don Pedro, and Leonato have been hidden to us by their courtly behavior. But it becomes clear that their failure to react humanely to Hero's plight results from wounded vanity on the one hand, and fear of "contamination" on the other. They are so angry at the loss of their reputations that they are more than half-convinced by Don John's word alone. Thus, later, we are not surprised that they have only to overhear a conversation in the dark between Borachio and Margaret, pretending to be Hero, to consider Hero's guilt established beyond doubt.

> *The street at night. Dogberry, with Verges, gives the Watch*
> *its instructions. All hide when people approach. Borachio*
> *tells Conrade what has just happened at Hero's window.*
> *The Watch overhear and arrest Conrade and Borachio*
> *(III.iii).*

Shakespeare enriches *Much Ado* with some of his most memorable low comedy characters, whom we now meet: the thick-headed Constable Dogberry and his inept crew of Watchmen. Dogberry murders the language with such gems as the outrageous instructions to the "most senseless and fit" men who make up the Watch (line 22). They may sleep while they are on duty, "for I cannot see how sleeping should offend" (line 40). The "most peaceable way" is not to "meddle or make" (lines 56, 51) with vagrants, drunkards, thieves, or delinquent nursemaids, for they must preserve the peace, offending no man, and this is best accomplished by making no arrests, as "it is an offence to stay a man against his will" (lines 79-80). They are to "comprehend all vagrom men" (lines 24-25), but they must let thieves alone, for "they that touch pitch will be defiled" (line 56). Dogberry's apparent idiocy parallels the equally irrational actions of the more intelligent people of the story.

He goes, and the Watch hides as the two assistant villains enter. "Seest thou not," Borachio says to Conrade,

> what a deformed thief this fashion is, how giddily 'a
> turns about all the hot bloods between fourteen and
> five-and-thirty, sometimes fashioning them like
> Pharaoh's soldiers in the reechy painting, sometime
> like god Bel's priests in the old church-window, some-
> time like the shaven Hercules in the smirched worm-
> eaten tapestry, where his codpiece seems as massy as his
> club?   (127-134)

That is, pride first creates the model soldier, gorgeously arrayed but overconfident and bent on vengeance as a means of gaining honour; then it supplies him with the outward attributes of one who cherishes a sacred trust, although he secretly abuses it; and finally it ushers in his destined role as an uxorious lover, tricked by appetite into an unmanly servitude which passes for devotion to his female captor. Pride signifies the image of one's self which one wishes to present to the public. Of course, it "is nothing to a man" (line 116), but in their ignorance all men are more concerned with the impression which they make on others than with their actual qualities of mind and spirit. Like a "deformed thief," fashion steals from men their knowledge of themselves, reducing them to posturing machines, who believe the illusion of their individuality while actually possessing none. They do not even choose the fashions they wear, which in fact are fashioned for them.

Before the arrest, the Watch creates one of the greatest illusions in theatre. When Borachio says to Conrade, "But seest though not what a deformed thief this fashion is?" one of the Watch whispers to another:

> I know that Deformed; 'a has been a vile thief this
> seven year; 'a goes up and down like a gentleman. I
> remember his name.   (122-124)

After the arrest, the Watch decides that "one Deformed is one of them; I know him, 'a wears a lock" (lines 163-164). As befits a majestically absurd creation, the idea of the villain Deformed keeps growing.

> *Hero is dressing for the wedding, helped by her women*
> *and Beatrice. Beatrice is subdued, and the others tease her:*
> *perhaps she is in love? (III.iv).*

> *Dogberry and Verges call on Leonato with some informa-*
> *tion but are unable to get to the point. Leonato, hurrying*
> *to the wedding, is exasperated. Dogberry says the Watch*
> *has "comprehended two aspicious persons" and want*
> *Leonato to examine them. He orders them to examine the*
> *men themselves (III.v).*

Don John's plot should be exposed and rendered impotent when Dogberry receives information about it. He and his partner, Verges, come to Leonato, the Governor, to report what has happened. Claudio and Don Pedro should be disabused of their false belief, and Hero should be spared her future trauma — if only Dogberry could deliver a simple message plainly, or if Leonato were not so preoccupied with his daughter's wedding. Clarity is not Dogberry's *forte*, and now he is intoxicated with the belief that he is engaged on an important mission. He becomes over-involved in a digression about protocol and rapidly exhausts Leonato's patience: "Neighbours, you are tedious," he exclaims (line 17). Dogberry, believing this an unusual compliment, graciously commends the Governor upon his spotless reputation and offers to present him with all his tediousness. When Verges tries to get the conversation back to the point, Dogberry is furious. He remarks caustically to Leonato that old men "will be talking" (forgetting whom he is addressing):

as they say, 'When the age is in, the wit is out.' God
help us, it is a World to see! *[To Verges]* Well said, i'faith,
neighbour Verges; well, God's a good man; *[To Leonato]*
an two men ride of a horse, one must ride behind. An
honest soul, i'faith, sir, by my troth he is, as ever broke
bread ...   (32-37)

Dogberry triumphs when Leonato, realizing that an affirmation
is required of him, says, "Indeed, neighbour, he comes too
short of you." Dogberry accepts this with reverent satisfaction:
"Gifts that God gives" (lines 39-40). Only now does he get to the
purpose of the interview. But it is too late. Leonato is off to the
wedding. He pauses just long enough to give Dogberry the task
he would normally undertake: the examination of the "two aspicious persons" whom the Watch has "comprehended" (line 43).

> At the church, Claudio returns Hero to her father, accus-
> ing her of being a wanton. Hero faints. The friar thinks
> Hero is innocent. She swears she met no one the night
> before. Benedick thinks the blame is with Don John.
> Leonato agrees to the friar's plan: he will say Hero has
> died of shame; this will cause Claudio to mourn her and
> may lead to the truth. Benedick and Beatrice declare their
> love. She asks him to kill Claudio. Benedick agrees to chal-
> lenge him (IV.i).

The next day Claudio publicly repudiates Hero at the altar:

There, Leonato, take her back again,
Give not this rotten orange to your friend;
She's but the sign and semblance of her honour.
Behold how like a maid she blushes here! ...
        Would you not swear,
All you that see her, that she were a maid
By these exterior shows? But she is none;
She knows the heat of a luxurious [lecherous] bed.
Her blush is guiltiness, not modesty.   (29-40)

"This looks not like a nuptial" (line 66), Benedick drily comments. Claudio stalks out of the church, and Hero swoons.

Claudio acts according to his role. During his eventful
courtship, he proudly takes a series of postures paralleling those
in Borachio's sketch of fashion's way with gallants. It is fashion
which converts Claudio's "soldier's eye" into one which quickly

notices "how fair young Hero is" (I.i.277, 283). Suddenly, deceived by Don John's trick, he transforms Hero from an exemplary and modest young woman into a wanton, like

>pampered animals
>That rage in savage sensuality. (58-59)

Claudio's rapid change in feelings from love to hate shows that he lacks both faith and charity. His hate does not change to remorse, although Friar Francis thinks it will "sweetly creep" into Claudio's "study of imagination" (lines 222-223).

Leonato is most enraged that Hero has tarnished his reputation — not a sympathetic reaction to a daughter's disgrace. As soon as he hears the accusation he wishes that she were not actually his flesh and blood:

>Why had I not with charitable hand
>Took up a beggar's issue at my gates,
>Who smirchèd thus and mired with infamy,
>I might have said 'No part of it is mine;
>This shame derives itself from unknown loins'?
>(129-133)

This kind of father is original to Shakespeare. None of his sources had ever written of such a father, who dwells on the insult to his dignity and ignores Hero's pain and possible innocence. His first thought when he learns of Hero's supposed depravity is of himself; and his second thought is of revenge. If Claudio and Don Pedro have wronged his daughter, Leonato says,

>Time hath not yet so dried this blood of mine,
>Nor age so eat up my invention,
>Nor fortune made such havoc of my means,
>Nor my bad life reft me so much of friends,
>But they shall find, awaked in such a kind,
>Both strength of limb and policy of mind,
>Ability in means and choice of friends
>To quit me of them throughly. (191-198)

Shakespeare makes Leonato a pawn of fashion: he avoids cost, and blusters about his position in society. Like Dogberry, he proclaims himself an ass.

This contrasts with Friar Francis. He sees at once that Hero is slandered; he is less concerned with vengeance than with restoring the faith of her friends. "Call me a fool," he says,

> Trust not my reading nor my observations,
> Which with experimental seal doth warrant
> The tenor of my book; trust not my age,
> My reverence, calling, nor divinity,
> If this sweet lady lie not guiltless here
> Under some biting error.   (162-168)

His powers are truly "gifts that God gives," for they come from dedication to his sacred calling. Friar Francis undertakes to "fashion the event" (line 233) that enables both Hero and Claudio to "die to live" (line 251), she by false death and the false identity of her cousin, he by penance.

No longer can Beatrice and Benedick play their previous roles. They gradually realize themselves in their new roles as mutual lovers. Beatrice is furious that Claudio and Don Pedro can pretend to be gentlemen when "manhood is melted into curtsies, valour into compliment, and men are only turned into tongue, and trim ones too" (lines 313-315). She hints she would be most thankful to the man who would right her cousin's wrong. Her ensuing dialogue with Benedick builds to a startling climax:

> BEN: By my sword, Beatrice, thou lovest me.
> BEA: Do not swear, and eat it.
> BEN: I will swear by it that you love me; and I will make him eat it that says I love not you.
> BEA: Will you not eat your word?
> BEN: With no sauce that can be devised to it; I protest I love thee.
> BEA: Why then, God forgive me!
> BEN: What offence, sweet Beatrice?
> BEA: You have stayed me in a happy hour; I was about to protest I loved you.
> BEN: And do it with all thy heart.
> BEA: I love you with so much of my heart that none is left to protest.
> BEN: Come, bid me do anything for thee.
> BEA: Kill Claudio.   (270-285)

This is a great *tour de force*, one of the finest in all theatre. It shocks both Benedick and the audience. Neither he nor we anticipate that the claims of love can be so bitter. Beatrice's demand is extreme, but her anger is free of the spite that erupts from injured pride (like Claudio). She has a real concern for her cousin's anguish and a genuine outrage at her accusers' self-righteousness: "O, on my soul, my cousin is belied!" (line 144), she says. Benedick demonstrates the effect of his love for Beatrice by joining Hero's side. This is ironic: the reformed misogynist suddenly becomes a knight-errant.

The Beatrice and Benedick plot is organically related to that of Claudio and Hero. Both are based on deception. Victimizers in one plot are the victims in the other, and vice versa. Claudio enters into the fun of fooling Benedick, unaware that he is to be fooled by Don John. The deceptions multiply as people exchange the roles of deceiver and deceived. The serious plot helps the romantic part of the play: Benedick must choose between Claudio and Beatrice; and the crisis in the Claudio-Hero plot brings the other courtship to a head. Deep feelings emerge momentarily but are always subordinate to comedy. Shakespeare contrasts the success of the relationship of the mature couple with the inadequacies of the younger pair. As Benedick has endured the worst of Beatrice, he cannot be shocked out of his love for her, even when she requires him to prove his love by killing his best friend. The irony is that this proof hinges on the lack of trust between the two innocent lovers, who cannot cope with a false challenge to their emotions.

The Third Movement: Complications

Dogberry, Verges, and the Sexton (town clerk) examine the prisoners, and the plot against Hero is exposed. Don John has fled. They take the prisoners to Leonato (IV.ii).

The hilarity of this famous scene is based on the interplay of the self-opinionated Dogberry, the aged Verges, the officious town clerk, and the Watch, as they try to legally examine Conrade and Borachio with superb incompetence. It is a great, if small, scene with a satiric purpose; the stupidity of using pride for personal revenge is emphasized by Dogberry's transformation from a man who would not willingly kill a dog into a fire-breathing nemesis for the villain who has dared to call him "ass."

The examination of Borachio and Conrade begins with

Dogberry's usual benign incompetence; indeed, if the Sexton does not intervene, it is likely that the prosecutor will find the defendants innocent. "Masters," he says, nearly inverting the usual procedures, "it is proved already that you are little better than false knaves, and it will go near to be thought so shortly" (lines 20-22). But when the prisoners deny the charge, Dogberry sees that they "are both in a tale" (lines 30-31) and, duly impressed by the coincidence, is about to make their self-styled innocence a matter of official record.

The Sexton completes the examination, records the confession of Borachio, and exits. The whole incident might end there, but Conrade objects to being taken in hand by Verges: "Off, coxcomb!" he exclaims. Then to Dogberry he says: "Away! You are an ass, you are an ass" (lines 67, 71). Dogberry's response deserves its reputation as one of the great comic angers: "Dost thou not suspect my place?" he asks, "Dost thou not suspect my years?" (lines 72-73). He is pained that the learned Sexton is no longer there to the record the infamous epithet which would condemn the villain who is "full of piety." But Conrade's crime will still be "proved upon [him] by good witness" (lines 76-77). Meanwhile, Dogberry's speech is a remarkable event:

> I am a wise fellow, and, which is more, an officer; and, which is more, a householder; and, which is more, as pretty a piece of flesh as any is in Messina; and one that knows the law, go to; and a rich fellow enough, go to; and a fellow that hath had losses; and one that hath two gowns and everything handsome about him. Bring him away. O that I had been writ down an ass! (77-84)

Dogberry, like Claudio, Leonato, and others in *Much Ado*, passionately defends any assault on his pride, on anything that, in fashionable terms, reduces him. His anger positively pulses with determination that its perpetrator shall not go unpunished. Dogberry even calls on his neighbours: "though it be not written down, yet forget not that I am an ass" (line 75).

Dogberry's function in the plot, with the assistance of his colleagues, is to uncover and report the evil of Don John and Borachio against Hero and Claudio. Dogberry delays this report, but once he knows the facts of Hero's innocence, the audience is set at ease about her; we know that the forces of law and order will prevail in the end. Dogberry has other significances in *Much Ado*. His catalogue of attributes which the world must note in order to appreciate the enormity of Conrade's slander is, in itself, a comic splendour; but it gains immensely in satiric point from its resemblance to the inventory made by Leonato on his own behalf (IV.i.191-198). Interestingly, the Duke in *Measure for Measure*, in testing his supposedly upright deputy, Angelo, might almost say with Dogberry that "The most peaceable way for you, if you do take a thief, is to let him show himself what he is and steal out of your company" (III.iii.56-58).

> *Leonato and Antonio have a furious argument with Don*
> *Pedro and Claudio over Hero. Benedick challenges*
> *Claudio to a duel, and tells Don Pedro that Don John has*
> *fled, and that he discontinues their friendship. Dogberry,*
> *Verges, and the Watch bring in their prisoners, and*
> *Borachio confesses everything. Don Pedro asks Leonato's*
> *forgiveness, and Claudio is stricken with remorse. Leonato*
> *requires Claudio to marry his niece in place of Hero and*
> *he agrees (V.i).*

With Leonato, as with most people in the world of *Much Ado*, moral responsibility is not subject to compulsion; if it does not occur spontaneously when it is needed, it does not occur. Men, he tells Antonio,

> Can counsel and speak comfort to that grief
> Which they themselves not feel; but, tasting it,
> Their counsel turns to passion, which before
> Would give preceptial medicine to rage,
> Fetter strong madness in a silken thread,
> Charm ache with air and agony with words.   (21-26)

As the Friar predicted, Leonato's anger has become remorse, restoring his faith in Hero. "My soul," he says, "doth tell me Hero is belied" (line 42). Dogberry (and Friar Francis) were correct: a thief, left to his own devices, will eventually show himself for what he is. Leonato was both a thief and a victim of thievery by allowing Don John to steal Hero's reputation; he robbed himself of his own better judgment. Now he has regained it: Hero's good reputation will follow when it is learned that Don John has fled from Messina "upon this vil-

lainy" (line 237). Antonio finds it futile to recommend that
Leonato suffer grief with patience:

> For there was never yet philosopher
> That could endure the toothache patiently....   (35-36)

But when Antonio suggests that his brother should "Make
those that do offend [him] suffer" (line 40), he gets a strong
reaction. Leonato challenges Claudio and Don Pedro, in all
seriousness, to mortal combat. Leonato and Antonio, oblivious
to their age, heap offensive provocation on the heads of the
able-bodied younger men.

Benedick's new-found belief in Hero's innocence brings
his rage to a fury. He challenges Claudio and Don Pedro (now
in his mind assassins) to the "trial of a man" (line 66). Don
Pedro is sarcastic when Benedick challenges Claudio to a duel:
"What a pretty thing man is," he says, "when he goes in his doublet and hose and leaves off his wit!" (lines 192-193). He recognizes pride in another, even if he cannot see it in himself.

With the theatrical timing of genius, Shakespeare chooses
this moment for the entrance of Dogberry, Verges, the Watch,
and their prisoners. Borachio confesses the whole plot.
Dogberry then urges upon Leonato the need to track down
Deformed, the criminal who has acquired (in Dogberry's imagination) even more marks of identification: "he wears a key in
his ear and a lock hanging by it" (lines 295-296). The fashion
of the dangling lovelock shows Deformed's excessive vanity.
Dogberry pictures Deformed as a confidence man, for he

> borrows money in God's name, the which he hath used
> so long and never paid, that now men grow hard-hearted
> and will lend nothing for God's sake.   (296-299)

"Pray you," Dogberry earnestly requests of Leonato, "examine
him upon that point" (line 299). In a miraculous way,
Shakespeare, through Dogberry, establishes an imaginary character whose personal pride makes himself and others suffer.
He is the perfect man of fashion: an illusion.

When performing Dogberry, I discovered (Leeds Art
Theatre Experimental Group, 1952) that he feels most satisfied
as he leaves the stage: he has preserved his enormous ego, and
he has done his duty well. Despite his bumbling incompetence,
his ponderous pride, and his incredible misuse of words (prefiguring Mrs. Malaprop by a century and a half), he is a perfec-

tionist. If we laugh at Dogberry, we share his blundering way of survival. His final words to Leonato are typical. "God save the foundation!" he exclaims (line 304), accepting Leonato's tip as if he is a charity. And wishing Leonato good health, he adds: "I humbly give you leave to depart; and if a merry meeting may be wished, God prohibit it!" (lines 310-312).

Leonato, Claudio and Don Pedro are reluctant to acknowledge that they have shown Hero a great lack of generosity; they prefer to believe that they have made a mistake. Although Shakespeare prepares us to accept Claudio's earlier actions as those of an immature and honourable young man, he has not prepared us for his willingness to marry, sight unseen, at Leonato's discretion. But Shakespeare must tie up the ends.

Beatrice and Benedick have an exchange of wit. Ursula tells them that Don John's plot is discovered (V.ii).

Don Pedro and Claudio visit Hero's monument in church, and Claudio hangs a scroll there, swearing he will perform this ritual every year (V.iii).

Throughout *Much Ado*, Shakespeare brilliantly juxtaposes scenes that are comic and serious, romantic and farcical. These are two quick scenes, the first sharp and witty, the second slow and serious. Then we are ready for the happy ending.

The Fourth Movement: Finale

As everyone gathers for the next wedding, Benedick asks Leonato for permission to marry Beatrice, which he gives. The women enter, masked, and Leonato refuses to let Claudio see the face of his new bride until he promises to marry her. He does, and Hero takes off her mask. Don John is reported captured, and all concludes with a dance (V.iv).

Shakespeare swiftly ties everything together so that the audience can go home well satisfied. Some critics, but not many audience members, think Claudio unworthy of his bride. His new love for her does not come from remorse but a change of judgment. Like Dogberry and other men of fashion, Claudio has blundered into the truth despite himself; after learning his mistakes, he concedes his failure publicly by accepting a new, unseen bride (his old one in disguise). Hero must accept a husband she knows callow and now dishonoured. It feels right that Claudio should marry a "resurrected" Hero: despite his faults, he is still the hero, and she seems content with him; and they marry only after attaining an awareness of their limitations — like Beatrice and Benedick earlier in the play.

The marriage of Beatrice and Benedick does not depend on naivety: they know each other's faults and marry from an affection that is "no more than reason," a mere "friendly recompense" (lines 77, 83). Their marriage may be stormy, yet it will survive. This is one of the few times in Shakespeare where both lovers are witty, worldly-wise, and unwilling to let their passions dominate them. The result is exhilarating in the theatre; at its best, it is breathtaking.

ROLES AND DISGUISE

Actors face a particular problem with *Much Ado*: they must distinguish between the personage and the personage's role. While this problem is common to all Shakespearean drama, in this play it is acute. The people who live in the world of *Much Ado* delight in human roles of all kinds. Indeed, the play consists almost entirely of their roles and playlets. For someone to survive, it is necessary to have good histrionic skills and sensibility: Beatrice's and Benedick's are good, but Claudio's are not. The modern actor, therefore, must convey to the audience that he or she is acting a theatrical personage who may, or may not, be acting a role, and may be acting a role well or badly.

But there are many other variants. Anyone may take a role for good or evil ends. A human "player" can be false or true. "Counterfeit" is a virtual synonym in Elizabethan English for the actor and his art and, thus, is often quite innocent. Antonio's sheepish "To tell you true, I counterfeit him" (II.i.103) is harmless. But villains like Borachio can also counterfeit others (e.g., Claudio) for evil purposes, and they can use disguise to do so.

In some cases, the idea of theatricality is used to suggest artificiality. Beatrice's mocking "Speak, Count, 'tis your cue" (II.i.281) recognizes artificiality in a situation that has no suggestion of a concealed audience. The theatrical nature of comic deceit is not necessarily dependent on disguise. In his arbour, Benedick supposes he is in the superior position of an audience overlooking the conversation of Claudio, Leonato, and Don Pedro about Beatrice's love for him. But he is, unknowingly, the central character of their playlet. A little later, Beatrice is forced into a similar position by the playlet of Hero, Ursula, and Margaret. Prior to this, as the women discuss with each other the way in which they will gull Beatrice, Hero and her gentlewoman adopt, quite naturally, the language of the theatre. Hero impresses upon Ursula that

> Our talk must only be of Benedick;
> When I do name him, let it be thy part
> To praise him more than ever man did merit.
>
> (III.i.17-19)

The only disguise involved here is verbal. However, the nature of the situation gives a specifically theatrical atmosphere to the familiar idiom "to play the part." This atmosphere becomes more vivid with Ursula's reply: "Fear you not my part of the dialogue" (III.i.31). A little later, Claudio says quite directly that "Hero and Margaret have by this played their parts with Beatrice, and then the two bears will not bite one another when they meet" (III.ii.69-71). Once the deception of Benedick is accomplished, Don Pedro looks forward to an even more delicious comedy: the meeting of Beatrice and Benedick. "That's the scene that I would see, which will be merely a dumb-show" (II.iii.213-214).

BEATRICE AND BENEDICK

Beatrice and Benedick must be ranked among Shakespeare's most dazzling people. Almost before we know it we are caught up in their "merry war":

> BEA: I wonder that you will still be talking, Signor
> Benedick; nobody marks you.
> BEN: What, my dear Lady Disdain! Are you yet living?
> BEA: Is it possible disdain should die while she hath
> such meet food to feed it as Signor Benedick?
> Courtesy itself must convert to disdain, if you
> come in her presence. (I.i.108-115)

Their exchanges of wit constitute a battle as verbally violent as any in Shakespeare's comedy. But they avoid the physical exchanges of *The Shrew,* and all ends in a complete acceptance of marriage — the hero's name has, in fact, become a synonym for "the married man."

Even before he enters, Beatrice has a disguised interest in his arrival. There is a hint of this interest in "they never meet but there's a skirmish of wit between them" (I.i.58): Shakespeare implies that Beatrice has had one affair with her "enemy." She usually gets the last word. "You have put him down, lady," Don Pedro says, "you have put him down." "So I would not he should do me, my lord, lest I should prove the mother of fools" (II.i.259-262) — a witty retort that suggests her interests. Benedick gives himself away when Claudio declares that Hero is the loveliest creature he has seen. Not so, says Benedick. "There's her cousin, an [if only] she were not possessed with a fury, exceeds her as much in beauty as the first of May doth the last of December" (I.i.178-180). Beatrice says to him that "You always end with a jade's trick; I know you of old" (I.i.136). Later, when told she has lost the heart of Benedick, she says sharply "Indeed, my lord, he lent it me awhile, and I gave him use for it, a double heart for his single one. Marry, once before he won it of me with false dice" (II.i.255-257). She implies he once gave her dishonest love in exchange for her innocent one, and that she is repaying him. Their friends think that "She were an excellent wife for Benedick" (II.i.325). The two have no illusions about each other, yet they are still attracted.

Like two of Shakespeare's earlier heroes, Valentine and Berowne, Benedick begins as "an obstinate heretic in the despite of beauty" (I.i.216-217) and ends as a lover. He laughs that he will never, like the lovesick Claudio, look pale with love: "With anger, with sickness, or with hunger, my lord, not with love" (I.i.229-230). What has happened to Claudio will not happen to him:

> I will not be sworn but love may transform me to an
> oyster; but I'll take my oath on it, till he have made an
> oyster of me, he shall never make me such a fool. One
> woman is fair, yet I am well; another is wise, yet I am
> well; another virtuous, yet I am well; but till all graces

> be in one woman, one woman shall not come in my
>   grace.   (II.iii.22-28)

His antipathy is so strong that he says of Beatrice "so, indeed,
all disquiet, horror, and perturbation follows her" (II.i.238-
239). Yet he makes a complete about-face. "Love me? Why, it
must be requited" (II.iii.218-219). He will be "horribly in love"
with her, even if teased about it:

> but doth not the appetite alter? A man loves the meat
> in his youth that he cannot endure in his age. Shall
> quips and sentences and these paper bullets of the
> brain awe a man from the career of his humour? No,
> the world must be peopled. When I said I would die a
> bachelor, I did not think I should live till I were mar-
> ried.   (II.iii.231-236)

Benedick tries to write poetry but gives up: "No, I was not born
under a rhyming planet, nor I cannot woo in festival terms"
(V.ii.39-40).

Beatrice, who speaks "all mirth and no matter" (II.i.305), is
grateful she has no husband and will never have one — at
least, not "till God make men of some other metal than
earth.... Adam's sons are my brethren, and, truly, I hold it a sin
to match in my kindred" [marry a relative] (II.i.52-57). An old
maid is supposed to lead apes to hell, but Beatrice will go no
farther than the gate:

> and there will the devil meet me, like an old cuckold
> with horns on his head, and say, "Get you to heaven,
> Beatrice, get you to heaven; here's no place for you
> maids." So deliver I up my apes, and away to Saint Peter
> for the heavens; he shows me where the bachelors sit,
> and there live we as merry as the day is long.
>   (II.i.37-43)

When Don Pedro playfully asks, "Will you have me, lady?" she
replies, "No, my lord, unless I might have another for working-
days: your grace is too costly to wear every day" (II.i.301-304).

She is tricked when she overhears Hero say, "Disdain and
scorn ride sparkling in her eyes" (III.i.51). Beatrice, who normally speaks the most buoyant prose, now puts her complex
emotions into formal rhymed verse:

> What fire is in mine ears? Can this be true?
>   Stand I condemned for pride and scorn so much?

Contempt, farewell! and maiden pride, adieu!
No glory lives behind the back of such.
And, Benedick, love on; I will requite thee,
Taming my wild heart to thy loving hand.
If thou dost love, my kindness shall incite thee
To bind our loves up in a holy band.
For others say thou dost deserve, and I
Believe it better than reportingly.   (III.i.107-116)

Like Benedick's, her about-face is quick. But in her case it is not an about-face at all; she loved him all the time.

Their game of wit has an important psychological and dramatic purpose. It allows them to fence through a mask of brilliant words, hiding their real feelings from everyone else, each other, and even themselves. The deceit over, they give way to their true emotions without losing face:

BEN: They swore that you were almost sick for me.
BEA: They swore that you were well-nigh dead for me.
BEN: 'Tis no such matter. Then you do not love me?
BEA: No, truly, but in friendly recompense.
                                                 (V.iv.80-83)

Each has written a "halting sonnet of his own pure brain":

BEN: A miracle! Here's our own hands against our
      hearts. Come, I will have thee; but, by this light,
      I take thee for pity.
BEA: I would not deny you; but, by this good day, I
      yield upon great persuasion; and partly to save
      your life, for I was told you were in a consumption.
BEN: *(Kissing her)* Peace! I will stop your mouth.
                                                 (V.iv.87, 91-97)

But their wit can be intensely serious. It clarifies their thinking: in all Messina, only they have the right intuition about Don John. "How tartly that gentleman looks!" Beatrice comments, "I never can see him but I am heart-burned an hour after" (II.i.3-4). When Hero is humiliated, Benedick knows that "The practice of it lives in John the Bastard" (IV.i.186). Their joint awareness of evil and genuine sympathy for Hero enables them to talk with an unaccustomed depth of feeling. It is a sign of Benedick's maturity that he continues to act even when he is ridiculous to his friends: "In brief, since I do purpose to marry, I will think nothing to any purpose that the world can say against it; for man is a giddy thing, and this is my conclusion" (V.iv.103-107).

These two cheerful egotists, for all their protestations, accept the fascinating idea that another loves them as they love themselves. Their sentimental love dominates *Much Ado*. There is little doubt that Beatrice and Benedick will create the happiest and sanest marriage in Shakespeare.

HERO AND CLAUDIO

The main hindrance to deep emotion is Claudio, whom literary critics have disliked for nearly everything he does: his wooing by proxy, his distrust of Don Pedro, his deception by Don John, his public repudiation of Hero, his flippant reception of Benedick's challenge, and his agreement to marry sight unseen. On stage, however, all these objections dissolve. In performance, the villainous Don John is entirely to blame; even his brother, Don Pedro, who is a reasonable man, is deceived. Anyone can make a mistake, but modern critics think Claudio lacks humanity in vengefully shaming Hero in public. Indeed, unless the actor playing Claudio understands that he is caught by the social view of pride and defilement, the role makes little sense. The influence of fashion in society and human interaction is a major target of the satire of *Much Ado*.

Claudio is a good match for Hero, who also tamely follows fashionable behaviour. She has a genteel complacency and is the perfect model of the fashionable ingénue, obedient to her father and apparently more concerned with the fashion of her wedding gown than with her feelings for the bridegroom, Claudio.

DOGBERRY

Dogberry is prouder than anyone, but he is not ambitious in a vulgar way. He is content to go about his daily business, enjoying what he thinks is his natural superiority. He is attentive to his duty (as he sees it), but he is the most permissive of officers. On the one occasion when his moral fury is roused, does not public decency demand harsh measures when a villain calls the most distinguished of "the poor Duke's officers" an "ass"? But normally he radiates a mild benevolence toward everyone. He is one of Shakespeare's greatest comic inventions. His inflated pride beams everywhere; he is exhilarated and joyful in his own accomplishments, combining the attitudes and flair of a great sage with the utterances and actions of a simpleton. Dogberry's aim is to be a model of virtuous conduct, particularly of Christian doctrine and morality. His instructions to the Watch may be nonsensical, but his frustrated anger at Conrade is understandable, if preposterous. It is the ultimate irony that he and his fellows should be the ones to unravel Don John's knavery. "What your wisdoms could not discover," Borachio confesses to Don Pedro, "these shallow fools have brought to light" (V.i.221-223).

Dogberry often appears to speak nonsense, as when he says that Borachio should, for his sins, "be condemned into everlasting redemption" (IV.ii.54-55). Perhaps he means "damnation" not "redemption," but Dogberry is not ignorant in an ordinary way. What he says has a kind of sense as he utters it, *in the performance:* it expresses his moral confusion. Being condemned into redemption is *not* nonsense. It is a familiar Christian paradox: e.g., the sinner's heart becomes a boon because it is drawn, like iron, to the magnet, God. Dogberry's remark is apt for Borachio, who shows signs of going straight. Dogberry is completely unaware of this. As Michael Polanyi might say, he knows more than he can say.* But Shakespeare knows the unconscious of his characters. Dogberry blunders into truth just as he blunders into everything. In his own words, we must recognize that "the eftest way" of getting at the point is some times to "go about" with it.

Dogberry is linked with Beatrice and Benedick in two ways. First, his unique use of language is an inversion of their word play. The pun in an altered context becomes the malapropism (or so-called Dogberryism), with its special kind of wisdom: e.g., "Is our whole dissembly appeared?" (IV.ii.1); "by this time our Sexton hath reformed Signor Leonato of the matter"

---

* Polanyi (1964).

(V.i.240-241); "Dost thou not suspect my place? Dost thou not suspect my years?" (IV.ii.72-73). Dogberry's stubbornly wrong-headed fascination with words reinforces the play's major theme of *hubris* (pride). Second, Dogberry helps keep the troubles of Claudio and Hero in comic perspective. The Watch uncovers Don John's villainy before the wedding, and it is only Dogberry's splendid "tediousness" that prevents Leonato from learning of it in time to set things right. But even as Claudio is shaming Hero in the church, we know that the "aspicious" Conrade and Borachio have been "comprehended" and are in prison awaiting "excommunication." Between Dogberry on the one hand and Beatrice and Benedick on the other, we cannot become too worried about the fate of the young lovers.

A major difference between Beatrice and Benedick and the Constable, however, does not appear on the printed page. Just as Dogberry reverses their word play, so, *on stage*, where they are sharp and quick like rapiers, Dogberry is slow and dull. He is the most gross example of the pride which is endemic to Messina. As I discovered in performance, the person of Dogberry requires a large and majestic, if ponderous, physical presence and a rhetorical emphasis of speech suited to a man who is quite, quite certain that he is just, merciful, wise, learned, handsome, witty, patriotic, wealthy, well-dressed and, above all, full of dignity. For Dogberry must impress the audience as a comic Everyman, an egotist whose self-assurance and self-ignorance go hand in hand.

THE COMEDY OF PRIDE

As a comedy that satirizes manners, *Much Ado* centers on human pride. Shakespeare peopled his play with characters who all, in one way or another, exemplify the infatuation of people with themselves. Leonato and Antonio, the two "old men" of the play, are Shakespeare's version of a pair of Pantalones from the *commedia dell'arte*. Both pride themselves on their youth. Leonato is progressively more foolish: his self-righteous indignation at Hero's supposed corruption becomes senile rage at her detractors, Claudio and Don Pedro. All three are deceived by Don John's plot and show themselves for what they are. At least Leonato seems to recognize that he has been at fault, although he does not acknowledge Hero's pain. Claudio and Don Pedro, obliged to admit that they have done Hero grave injustice, rationalize their action:

> yet sinned I not
> But in mistaking. (V.i.261-262)

They appear to be incorrigible, just as Dogberry is proof against the smallest glimmer of self-knowledge. The inference is that we all over-rationalize — in Shakespeare's mind, it is the human condition.

Don John prides himself on his evil as much as Dogberry does on his benevolence. Like Dogberry, Don John is a bumbler who relishes "mortifying mischief." Despite his protestations of evil, he fails even in his little plot. But Borachio is different: he deceives people, not because he is a dedicated villain like Don John, but because villainy is easy and well paid. The question, as he points out to Conrade, is why "villainy should be so rich" (III.iii.110).

There remains Deformed who, although he is never visible, becomes a leading person in the play. From the moment that a nameless member of Dogberry's eavesdropping Watch is inspired (III.iii.116), in the minds of the Watch a metaphor becomes a thing of flesh and blood. Deformed, it seems, "has been a vile thief this seven year," and what is still more shocking, "'a goes up and down like a gentleman" (III.iii.123-124). No wonder, then, that the Watch is hot on his trail, or that Dogberry sees his destiny as the adversary of Deformed. Perhaps the greatest stroke of Shakespeare's comic art is that the capture of Deformed depends on pride.

AS YOU LIKE IT

We are always amazed at Shakespeare's bravery when we work with his plays in the theatre. The man is a risk-taker. But he understands theatrical issues so well that his judgment is superb.

Nowhere is his genius more obvious than in *As You Like It*. This famous comedy is so well-known, and Rosalind is so well-loved, we may forget that *As You Like It* has a daring and brilliant two-fold design. First, Shakespeare puts all the dramatic tension and action in Act I. Later we are transported to the forest of Arden where there is little tension and absolutely no physical action. Then Shakespeare, with a sweep of his hand that takes our breath away, resolves the whole plot with a multiple wedding. And second, it is a charming and delightful play only on the surface. *As You Like It* appears to be Shakespeare's gentlest and kindest comedy; it plays radiant happiness upon wistful melancholy, and the whole shines on Rosalind, one of Shakespeare's miracles. Yet it hides a difficult issue that he addresses head-on: the place of women in society. The result is one of his most popular plays.

THE GENTLE COMEDY

In Bernard Shaw's *The Dark Lady of the Sonnets*, Shakespeare says to Queen Elizabeth: "I have also stole from a book of idle wanton tales two of the most damnable foolishnesses in the world, in the one of which a woman goeth in man's attire and maketh impudent love to her swain, who pleaseth the groundlings by overthrowing a wrestler.... I have writ these to save my friends from penury, yet shewing my scorn for such follies and for them that praise them by calling the one *As You Like It*, meaning that it is not as I like it." The play makes its own ironic comment on those who say such things: "You have said; but whether wisely or no, let the forest judge."

The play wafts romance over us: there is a handsome young

hero, two princesses in disguise to be wooed, and a good but banished Duke to be restored to his rightful throne. The play radiates delight. But compared with Shakespeare's other comedies, it lacks extreme contrasts; even the two villains are not too evil and easily repent. Shakespeare brilliantly establishes the initial tension between court and forest. Once in Arden this tension recedes and there is little physical action. The forest abounds in "dislocating confrontations" or "juxtapositions," but they are not violent oppositions. Nor is there much broad humour. The result is a unified whole where cruder humours would be out of place.

As You Like It is a comedy that is very near to the old rituals from which drama and theatre came. "The sacred marriage" of ancient cultures celebrated fertility and procreation, the rebirth of the cosmos and the land, performed in a ritual drama. In comedy the young marry to become the older generation, whose children marry, and so *ad infinitum* — what Rosalind calls "the full stream of the world." Comic plots have coincidences, changes, and surprises, but never death like the ancient ritual battle of summer and winter. Shakespeare alters his source: Charles the wrestler does not kill his opponents; the wicked Duke is not killed in battle — improbably he becomes a hermit. But improbability is part of comedy. *As You Like It* is an allusive play uniting many old traditions (including a procession with deer going back to hunting rituals and folk plays), songs, impressive spectacles, a wrestling match, and the Masque of Hymen to end with courtly grace and dignity.

BACKGROUND TO THE PLAY

As You Like It was first published in the 1623 Folio but was probably written in early 1600. The play owes much to the pastoral tradition. Greek poets idealized shepherds and country life from the third century B.C.: innocent shepherds tend their flocks and fall in love with beautiful girls to whom they write anguished verse. Pastoralism was popular in the Renaissance: in Edmund Spenser's poem *The Shepherds Calendar* (1579) and Sir Philip Sidney's prose epic *Arcadia* (1590) it produced major literary works; other writers gave courtiers elegant escapist literature with conventional moralizing — *The Two Gentlemen* is based on one pastoral story.

Shakespeare's immediate source for *As You Like It* is Thomas Lodge's pastoral romance, *Rosalynde* or *Euphues Golden Legacie* (printed 1590), based on a short, medieval narrative poem; Lodge adds several stories, and Shakespeare takes them over. *Rosalynde* mixes folk tale, pastoral love eclogue, and pastoral romance, in the highly mannered style of Euphuism — made popular by John Lyly in the 1570s but here relieved by homeliness. Shakespeare follows Lodge's plot and develops many of its situations. The title probably comes from Lodge, who in a note to his "gentlemen readers" says, "If you like it, so." Orlando is gentler than Lodge's hero; indeed, it has been said that Shakespeare's hero is a Hercules-Christ figure with Christian forgiveness in his behaviour toward Oliver. There is no direct evidence that Shakespeare draws on any other work, but he probably knew two Robin Hood plays performed in 1598 by the Admiral's Company that may have suggested the outlaws, and *Sir Clyomon and Clamydes* (printed in 1599) may have led to Audrey and William.

As You Like It is like ancient pastorals with different forms: the pastoral romance of two princesses who play at being a shepherd boy (Ganymede) and his sister; the pastoral love-eclogue of Phebe's wooing (burlesqued in Audrey's wooing); and the moral eclogue where Corin the shepherd is wise. Arden forest is a pastoral retreat where "many young gentlemen ... fleet the time carelessly as they did in the golden world" (I.i.110-112). Shakespeare also delicately satirizes the pastoral ideal. The exiled Duke wishes to live in harmony with Nature and says his followers are lucky to be freezing because that is better for the soul than life at court:

> And this our life, exempt from public haunt,
> Finds tongues in trees, books in the running brooks,
> Sermons in stones, and good in everything.
> I would not change it.   (II.i.15-18)

As Rosalind and her companions arrive at Arden, they find clichés of pastoral romance. Silvius, a stereotypical lovesick shepherd, describes his agonies to an old shepherd, Corin, who in his youth must have "sighed upon a midnight pillow" (II.iv.23) even as Silvius sighs now:

> If thou rememberest not the slightest folly
> That ever love did make thee run into,

Thou hast not loved.
Or if thou hast not sat as I do now,
Wearing [tiring] thy hearer in thy mistress' praise,
Thou hast not loved.
Or if thou hast not broke from company
Abruptly, as my passion now makes me,
Thou hast not loved.
O Phebe, Phebe, Phebe! *[Exit.]*   (II.iv.30-39)

This reminds the earthy Touchstone of how he acted as a lover:

I remember when I was in love I broke my sword upon
a stone and bid him take that for coming a-night to
Jane Smile, and I remember the kissing of her batler
[bat used to pound clothes during washing] and the
cow's dugs that her pretty chopt [chapped] hands had
milked; and I remember the wooing of a peascod
instead of her, from whom I took two cods and, giving
her them again, said with weeping tears, 'Wear these
for my sake.' We that are true lovers run into strange
capers....   (II.iv.42-50)

Ganymede meets the shepherdess who has reduced Silvius to misery. S/he advises, "Sell when you can, you are not for all markets" (III.v.60).

Shakespeare ridicules the pastoral in the bumpkins Audrey and William, an earthy contrast to the artificial shepherds. "Truly," Touchstone says to Audrey, "I would the gods had made thee poetical." "I do not know what 'poetical' is," she replies. "Is it honest in deed and word? Is it a true thing?" (III.iii.13-16). He wins her, but Touchstone has no illusions about his motive: "so man hath his desires; and as pigeons bill, so wedlock would be nibbling" (III.iii.73-74). He is happy to get married, to "press in here ... amongst the rest of the country copulatives" (V.iv.53-54).

The stage history of the play is chequered. Charles Johnson's *Love in a Forest*, a version with passages from other Shakespeare plays, played at Drury Lane in 1723. Eighteen years later an edited version of *As You Like It* appeared, but Shakespeare's full text waited another century before it was performed. In the late nineteenth century, Ellen Terry made Rosalind her own, and, despite many major modern productions of the play, only Katherine Hepburn has rivalled "E.T."

The production we would all have wished to see was in the open air at St. Louis (1916) with the Rosalind of Margaret Anglin and the Touchstone of Sydney Greenstreet.*

THE FOREST OF ARDEN

The play's core lies in Arden. This green world is the reverse of the court: court-forest is the play's first double structure. Arden recalls the wood in *The Dream* and Prospero's island. It is set apart, but, unlike them, it is not magical. The changes that happen here are natural: the result of living close to Nature, the greenwood of Robin Hood. The contrast is a tyrant's envious court. Although Arden is utterly free, it has a strong parental presence. Duke Senior calls his companions "brothers" (II.i.1), but he is no democrat. He dispenses favour on a hierarchical basis:

Shall share the good of our returnèd fortune

According to the measure of their states. (V.iv.171-172)

Although *As You Like It* stresses youthful love, it occurs in a paternal context. Both Rosalind and Orlando acknowledge Duke Senior. Rosalind says "My father loved Sir Rowland [Orlando's father] as his soul" (I.ii.223), and thus her affection is compatible with family approval.

The forest at first appears untouched by life's discontents. Before entering, Celia sees it as an opportunity for freedom:

Now go in we content

To liberty, and not to banishment.   (I.iii.135-136)

But Corin's master is churlish, Sir Oliver Martext is unpleasant, William is stupid, Audrey graceless, and Arden has a bitter winter. To Orlando it is "this uncouth forest" (II.vi.6) and a desert where the air is bleak. Rosalind's "Well, this is the Forest of Arden" is not enthusiastic; and Touchstone says, "Ay, now am I in Arden, the more fool I. When I was at home I was in a better place, but travellers must be content" (II.iv.12-15). Nature's laws are not forgotten. In the world, Duke Frederick usurped Duke Senior, who has usurped the deer, the forest's natives. For Jaques, the callousness of Nature mirrors that of men: the

---

* For stage history see Barnet (1987), Salgado (1975), Sprague (1944, 1953), and Sprague and Trewin (1970).

herd abandons the wounded deer. Orlando, wanting help for
Adam, sees Nature as *nurture:*

> Then but forbear your food a little while
> Whiles, like a doe, I go to find my fawn
> And give it food. There is an old poor man
> Who after me hath many a weary step
> Limped in pure love; till he be first sufficed,
> Oppressed with two weak evils, age and hunger,
> I will not touch a bit.   (II.vii.128-134)

At times Arden seems to be a place where the same bitter
lessons can be learned as Lear must learn on the blasted heath.
Corin's natural knowledge that "the property of rain is to wet"
is what Lear must painfully acquire:

> When the rain came to wet me once and the wind to
> make me chatter when the thunder would not peace at
> my bidding, there I found 'em, there I smelt 'em out.
> Go to, they are not men o' their words. They told me I
> was everything. 'Tis a lie, I am not ague-proof.
>   (*Lear,* IV.vi.100-105)

He echoes Duke Senior who, of the "icy fang and churlish
chiding of the winter's wind," says:

> 'This is no flattery; these are counsellors
> That feelingly persuade me what I am.'   (II.i.10-11)

Amiens's lovely melancholy song:

> Blow, blow, thou winter wind,
> Thou art not so unkind
> As man's ingratitude ...   (II.vii.175-178)

is terribly echoed in Lear's outburst: "Blow, winds, and crack
your cheeks!" (*Lear,* III.ii.1). And Jaques's reflection that "All
the world's a stage" becomes in Lear's mouth a cry of anguish:

> When we are born, we cry that we are come
> To this great stage of fools.   (*Lear,* IV.vi.183-184)

Arden is the place of contradiction and paradox. One person's view differs from another's, so that the whole play is of
multiple understandings: e.g., sweet vs. sour, cynical vs. idealistic, hard fortune vs. good luck. In Arden, "most friendship is
feigning, most loving mere folly" is twice repeated; and Jaques
presents his joyless picture of human life, from futility to senili-
ty, "sans everything." Orlando enters with Adam in his arms; he
may be "sans teeth," but he has his virtue, his peace of con-

science, and the love of his master. Jaques has left out love, companionship, and the banquet to which Duke Senior welcomes Orlando and Adam. Arden is where people can find happiness in themselves and in others.

In Arden, everyone can discover truth and find himself through errors and mistakes (in disguisings). Misunderstanding leads people to understand; *by fiction, they discover truth.* This is the focus of the play. Rosalind, as Ganymede playing Rosalind, can tax her lover Orlando to the limit, only to discover that she cannot drive him "to forswear the full stream of the world, and to live in a nook merely monastic" (III.ii.400-402). By playing with him in the disguise of a boy, she discovers when she can play no more. Phebe, by loving a shadow, discovers that it is better to love than to be loved and scorn one's lover. It is a play of human interactions: Orlando-Jaques, Touchstone-Corin, Rosalind-Jaques, Rosalind-Phebe, and Rosalind-Orlando. The truth discovered is the "earthy truth" of fertility: the honest toil of the wise Corin is mocked by Touchstone as "simple sin"; he brings "the ewes and the rams together" and gets his living "by the copulation of cattle." Touchstone's marriage to Audrey is a simple coupling. Rosalind's words to describe Oliver and Celia "in the very wrath of love" (V.ii.38) are blunt, and her own sighs are for her "child's father" (I.iii.11). In this forest human love cannot "forget the He and She." But Rosalind's behaviour is different from her bold words: Orlando must prove that he is the right husband for her. This is the true marriage of the play, and the others are variations, including Touchstone's vivid image of "a she-lamb of a twelve month" and "a crooked-pated, old, cuckoldy ram" (III.ii.77-78). And we learn that "minds innocent and quiet" can find happiness in court or country:

> Happy is your grace
> That can translate the stubbornness of fortune
> Into so quiet and so sweet a style. (II.i.18-20)

But those who wish can "suck melancholy" out of anything, "as a weasel sucks eggs" (II.v.11-12).

THE PLAY METAPHOR

In exile in the forest of Arden, the Duke reminds the banished
lords of the comparative ease of the roles they have in the theatre of the world:

> Thou seest we are not all alone unhappy.
> This wide and universal theatre
> Presents more woeful pageants than the scene
> Wherein we play in.   (II.vii.137-140)

Jaques seizes the metaphor and makes it memorable. The idea
of the world as a stage populated by actors is everywhere in
Shakespeare, but two famous examples are formal play
metaphors, moral in tone, when the dramatic action stops.
First is Jaques's famous observations on the subject:

> All the world's a stage,
> And all the men and women merely players ...
>   (II.vii.140-141)

Mixing this with the traditional theme of the seven ages of
man, Jaques provides a sense of futility common to many
Elizabethan stage metaphors. Second is the meditative comment of Antonio in *The Merchant:*

> I hold the world but as the world, Gratiano —
> A stage, where every man must play a part,
> And mine a sad one.   (*The Merchant,* I.i.77-79)

In neither is the reflection cheerful.

Rosalind, recovering from her unmanly swoon and trying
to make it look like jest, centres her conversation with Oliver
upon "counterfeit":

> ROS: Counterfeit, I assure you.
> OL: Well then, take a good heart, and counterfeit to
>   be a man.
> ROS: So I do; but, i'faith, I should have been a
>   woman by right.   (IV.iii.171-175)

On the stage, Rosalind *is* the metaphor: a boy playing Rosalind
playing Ganymede playing Rosalind. Jan Kott says that, in the
original production, this was rich in sexual ambiguity:
"Everything is real and unreal, false and genuine at the same
time";* the meaning of disguise in the Renaissance was to sepa-

---

* Kott (1967).

rate eroticism from the limitations of the body; it was a dream of love free from the limitations of sex, of love pervading the bodies of males and females. Corin's invitation to Rosalind and Celia leads us to the more unrealistic dialogue of Silvius and his disdainful love:

> If you will see a pageant truly played,
> Between the pale complexion of true love
> And the red glow of scorn and proud disdain,
> Go hence a little and I shall conduct you,
> If you will mark it.   (III.iv.47-51)

But there is a deeper meaning to the metaphor. Rosalind in the clothing of Ganymede (androgyny — one level of illusion) challenges the male world of Duke Senior (Christian — a second level of illusion), an issue less easily resolved.

Even with such a serious subtext, however, it is the most exquisite of the comedies, with a superb theatrical quality that gives even minor scenes great appeal.

STRUCTURE AND PLOT

In *As You Like It* Shakespeare returns to the pattern of *The Dream*, beginning his play in sorrow and ending it with joy, while making his comic locality a place apart from the ordinary world. He uses three structures:

[1]   *The linear and temporal structure is three-fold:* the court, the forest, and the finale — the Movements of the play. Once again we are forced to abandon the Act and scene divisions of editors working long after Shakespeare's death.

[2]   *The spatial structure is two-fold:* the "double" metaphoric meanings (e.g., person-role, male-female, truth-fiction, world-theatre, face-mask, forest-court, love-sex, youth-age) are symbolically expressed as love, empathy, and Nature vs. power, envy, and city life.

[3]   *The deep structure is male-female:* how can women in Elizabethan society control their lives? This is revealed by the other structures and the plot.

The plot tells of the lack of responsibility of an elder brother for a younger (Oliver for Orlando) and the lack of respect a younger brother has for an elder (Duke Frederick for Duke

Senior). The plot unfolds with extraordinary speed. Almost all the events occur in the First Movement (Act I): attempted murder, cracked ribs, and people escaping to the forest. Then, in the Second Movement (II.i-V.iii), the play stands almost still; the interest is not intended to arise out of the action or situation. Except for tiny scenes we are always in Arden, where the chief dangers are to fall in love or lose in debate. Shakespeare addresses two enduring human illusions: the pastoral ideal and the ideal of romantic love. The Third Movement (V.iv), the finale, ties everything up. The two villains are said to have been converted, and four pairs of lovers are to be married. But there are some inconsistencies of plot: the length of time that Duke Senior has been banished to the forest; and the appearance at the end of the play of one "Jaques" (the middle son of Sir Rowland), whose speeches are marked "Second Brother" — and yet a second Jaques is a major character in the play. Such problems are not unusual in actors' working scripts.

THE ACTION

The First Movement: The Court

The good Duke Senior, usurped by his younger brother Frederick, lives with a few courtiers in the forest of Arden. Orlando, son of the late Sir Rowland de Boys, is mistreated by his older brother Oliver, who holds his inheritance (I.i).

The opening of *As You Like It* is brilliant — as superb in comedy as the start of *Hamlet* is in tragedy. Both prefigure the rest of the play. Like Henry de Montherlant's *Malatesta, As You Like It* opens with a fight. "The spirit of my father, which I think is within me, begins to mutiny against this servitude," Orlando tells old Adam (lines 20-21). Orlando's naturalness comes from the training provided by his brother. "He keeps me rustically at home," Orlando tells Adam.

When Oliver enters, Orlando complains to him, "you have trained me like a peasant, obscuring and hiding from me all gentleman-like qualities" (lines 64-65) and demands to be taught them. (Later, Touchstone makes fun of such gentlemanly education as poison, bastinado, faction, and policy, just as

Oliver shows them in practice.) The irony of Orlando's demand, like the irony of his competing with Charles, saves him from becoming a male stereotype: he is neither corrupted nor corruptible.

Orlando brawls with Oliver: a symbolic encounter between love and power. "Wilt thou lay hands on me?" Oliver cries. "Wert thou not my brother," says Orlando, "I would not take this hand from thy throat." Who strikes first? Probably Oliver, but we cannot be certain. *"Going to strike"* is written by some early actor in a copy of the 1794 acting edition. Tradition has Adam try to help Oliver to his feet, which is the pretext for Oliver's "Get you with him, you old dog." (line 76). Orlando asserts the paternal bond: "The spirit of my father grows strong in me, and I will no longer endure it" (lines 65-66). His dead father gives him his sense of identity, as yet unfulfilled.

Charles, the professional wrestler, tells Oliver of the overthrow of the old Duke and his banishment: there is discord in both the public and private life of the state, of which the wrestling match is a symbol. Charles, as jealous of his position as any courtier, says to Oliver:

> Tomorrow, sir, I wrestle for my credit, and he that
> escapes me without some broken limb shall acquit him
> well. Your brother is but young and tender, and for
> your love I would be loath to foil him, as I must for my
> own honour if he come in.   (118-123)

> *The good Duke's daughter, Rosalind, remains at Court
> with her friend Celia, Frederick's daughter. When Orlando
> challenges the wrestler Charles, Oliver hopes his brother
> will be maimed or killed. But Orlando defeats Charles, to
> the chagrin of Oliver but to the relief and delight of the two
> young women (I.ii).*

Celia declares the love she has for Rosalind, thereby creating a redemptive time:

> You know my father hath no child but I, nor none is
> like to have; and truly, when he dies, thou shalt be his
> heir: for what he hath taken away from thy father per-
> force, I will render thee again in affection.   (16-19)

The wrestling match is the symbolic focus of the First Movement. As Shaw said, it might have pleased the ground-

lings, but it is simultaneously a graphic image for discord: servi-
tude vs. freedom, Orlando vs. Oliver, Frederick vs. Rosalind.
Orlando and Charles each represent various aspects of the
play's themes when they finally meet. Charles has accepted
Oliver's false report of Orlando's treachery — "this wrestler,"
Oliver says, "shall clear all" (I.i.159-160).

Charles, the champion of the court and of Oliver, and
Orlando, the champion of Nature and pastoral ideals, meet in
a ritual battle: Orlando's traditional male rite of passage, an
appropriate form for the violence he expressed in the fight
with Oliver. Shakespeare usually condemns aggression as a
basis for love; but here it simply shows the methods of the
tyrant, Frederick. (Eventually Orlando must give up violence to
join Duke Senior, his father-symbol.) Orlando embodies the
values of Nature: an alternative, more peaceful, less competi-
tive life style. He stands for the forest: his surname (originally
de Bois) shows he is the son of Sir Rowland — the inheritor of
the greenwood, of earthly fertility. The movement of the whole
play ritualizes the seasonal change from the wrestling match
(ritual of chaos-death), to the forester's march with the slain
deer (ritual of invigoration), and to the harmony of the weddings and dances with which the play ends (a fertility ritual
dance-feast.)*

Orlando's first step is the demolition of Charles the
wrestler:

How dost thou, Charles?
He cannot speak, my lord.   (206-207)
His victory allows Orlando to claim his father's name:
DUKE F:What is thy name, young man?
ORL: Orlando, my liege the youngest son of Sir
          Rowland de Boys ... I am more proud to be Sir
          Rowland's son.   (209-211, 220)
Frederick reacts negatively to Orlando's heritage:
Thou shouldst have better pleased me with this deed
Hadst thou descended from another house.   (215-216)
The wrestling scene shows that comic time governs the
play: it can alter normal causation. Power, reason, and abstrac-

---

* The ancient tradition of ritual dramas to celebrate seasonal change is
described by Gaster (1961).

tion can be upset by love, imagination, and natural experience: "accidents" like Orlando throwing Charles, who should have won, abound. Most have no reason to happen, but Orlando's success has a reason *not* to happen.

Is Orlando worthy of Rosalind? This question has occupied the critics and it needs to be addressed by both reader and director. She is clearly the initiator of their relationship in this Movement. In a thinly disguised rehearsal for the future wedding, Rosalind claims her share of the victory by ironically placing a chain around Orlando's neck. "Wear this for me — one out of suits with fortune" (line 234). His perceptions and hers are much alike, and their naturalness contrasts with the rigidity of Duke Frederick. But not even Rosalind can always see beyond appearance: "Pray heaven, I be deceived in you!" she says to him (line 184). She is.

> *Fearful of his niece's popularity, Duke Frederick banishes Rosalind, who has fallen in love with Orlando as Orlando has with her; she flees with Celia, both in disguise (I.iii).*

When Frederick exiles Rosalind, he relies on temporal terms for force:

DUKE F. Mistress, dispatch you with your safest
                haste
         And get you from our court.
ROSALIND Me, uncle?
DUKE F. You, cousin.
         Within these ten days if that thou beest
                found
         So near our public court as twenty miles,
         Thou diest for it.   (38-43)

The threat is repeated later in case it is missed: "If you outstay the time, you die." But Oliver's unkindness to Orlando and Frederick's enmity to Rosalind do not affect us too deeply; they are devices to ensure that the lovers meet in the forest, where the main interest of the play lies.

Rosalind adopts the male disguise of Ganymede and sets out for Arden forest, accompanied by Celia, in the role of Ganymede's sister Aliena, and by the court jester, Touchstone. Shakespeare is in great haste to get his characters into the forest of Arden. This may account for some confusions: the heights of Rosalind and Celia, the ages of the two Dukes, and the time since Frederick usurped the throne. But these discrepancies do not harm the brilliance of the opening Movement of *As You Like It.*

The Second Movement: The Forest

We are introduced to Duke Senior and his lords in the forest of Arden. Meanwhile, two parties arrive in Arden: Rosalind, Celia and Touchstone; and Orlando and the old servant Adam fleeing from Oliver. Apart from brief glimpses of the court, the rest of the play takes place in the forest of Arden (II.i-II.v).

In a clearing, Duke Senior addresses the lords who live with him in the forest (II.i), and his attendant Amiens praises his ability to translate misery into pleasant rhetoric. Shakespeare establishes a male caring society where the feast "feelingly persuades me what I am" (II.i.11). "Sweet are the uses of adversity" because, as Orlando is to discover, adversity disappears when men's "gentleness" prevails. It can

> translate the stubbornness of fortune
> Into so quiet and sweet a style.   (II.i.19-20)

This explains why "loving lords have put themselves into voluntary exile" with the Duke and why "many young gentlemen flock to him every day" (I.i.95-96, 110-111). In an ironic comment upon Duke Senior's speech, we hear that a deer weeping into a stream gave Jaques a chance for ludicrous moralizing.

Back at court, we know more of Orlando when Adam says:

> O my sweet master, O you memory
> Of old Sir Rowland, why, what make you here?
> Why are you virtuous? Why do people love you?
> And wherefore are you gentle, strong, and valiant? ...
> O, what a world is this, when what is comely
> Envenoms him that bears it!   (II.iii.3-15)

Adam explicitly says Oliver does not behave like Sir Rowland's son:

> within this roof
> The enemy of all your graces lives....
> Yet not the son, I will not call him son
> Of him I was about to call his father....   (II.iii.17-21)

Rosalind lacks enthusiasm when she, Celia, and Touchstone reach Arden:

> O Jupiter, how weary are my spirits! ... I could find in
> my heart to disgrace my man's apparel, and to cry like
> a woman.... Well, this is the Forest of Arden. (II.iv.1-12)

She meets Corin, the old shepherd who is so much a part of Nature that he cannot utter an unsound word or do an ungenerous deed. Celia says "I like this place; And willingly could waste my time in it" (II.iv.91-92).

Orlando's initiation to the forest is similar, but Rosalind and Orlando approach the forest with different aims. Rosalind's mission is love, and she discovers the love she has brought with her:

> Alas, poor shepherd, searching of thy wound,
> I have by hard adventure found mine own. (II.iv.40-41)

Orlando, escaping from his brother, has two implicit aims in the forest: to re-establish the link with his father's legacy and to make a quest for Rosalind. When Adam, like Celia, "can go no further," Orlando sees an "uncouth forest," a "desert." The air, he says, is "bleak." Adam collapses from lack of food. Orlando treats it as another trial of "the strength of my youth," an "adventure" like the wrestling match. "If this uncouth forest yield anything savage, I will either be food for it or bring it for food to thee" (II.vi.6-7). The younger man acts as a father to the older.

> *Orlando is led to Duke Senior's pastoral banquet which he*
> *enters with drawn sword (II.vii).*

He finds his rude demands answered by natural hospitality. Like Rosalind, Orlando finds he is playing a part to protect himself:

> Speak you so gently? Pardon me, I pray you.
> I thought that all things had been savage here,
> And therefore put I on the countenance
> Of stern commandment.   (107-110)

The Duke confirms Orlando's identity with virtually a ritual blessing:

> ORL: If ever you have looked on better days;
>   If ever been where bells have knolled to
>   church;

> If ever sat at any good man's feast;
> If ever from your eyelids wiped a tear,
> And know what 'tis to pity and be pitied....
> DUKE: True is it that we have seen better days,
> And have with holy bell been knolled to
> church,
> And sat at good men's feasts, and wiped our
> eyes
> Of drops that sacred pity hath engendered....
> (114-118, 121-124)

Their father-son relation, linked imaginatively with the image of Orlando carrying Adam on his back and sustaining him with food, is the basis for future social cohesion. Unexpectedly finding a benevolent father figure, Orlando effects a graceful transition from aggression to tenderness:

> Let gentleness my strong enforcement be,
> In the which hope I blush, and hide my sword.
> (119-120)

This display of non-violence brings Orlando into the male society of Arden. He goes to fetch Adam while Jaques entertains the Duke and his lords with his "All the world's a stage" speech. Implicitly symbolic is love = food: this becomes explicit later in the wedding scene. Men have society's nurturant roles, which are traditionally maternal. Duke Senior's patriarchal abundance of food and of "gentleness" creates an image of a self-sustaining male system in Arden.

Orlando returns, bearing his "venerable burden." Duke Senior sees the father's reflection in the son and declares his own loving connection with Sir Rowland. From now on, Duke Senior plays "father" to Orlando's "son":

> If that you were the good Sir Rowland's son,
> As you have whispered faithfully you were,
> And as mine eye doth his effigies witness
> Most truly limned and living in your face,
> Be truly welcome hither. I am the Duke
> That loved your father. (195-200)

Arden is defined by time. In contrast, Touchstone is Fortune's timepiece. His famous "And so from hour to hour we ripe, and ripe, And then from hour to hour we rot, and rot" (lines 26-27) is related with approval by Jaques, who has his own view of time, the "seven ages." Touchstone's time closely resembles the Court's time because Duke Frederick rules by the clock. Jaques dissolves the distinctions between court and forest by seeing them pessimistically; Touchstone dissolves them through his realism.

> *Frederick, furious that Celia, Rosalind and Orlando have fled, threatens Oliver unless he finds his brother (III.i).*

Duke Frederick tells Oliver to produce his brother

Within this twelvemonth, or turn thou no more

To seek a living in our territory.   (7-8)

Time is inflexible and threatening for the court, the realist, and the cynic: like Fortune's wheel, its movement is inexorable and destructive. In another context, it would be tragic: it leads to death. The natural time of Arden, on the other hand, is comic: opposition to clock time leads to life.

> *In Arden, Orlando meets Rosalind as a boy (Ganymede), and "he" acts the role of Rosalind so Orlando can practise wooing her. From then on, wonders happen: the shepherdess Phebe, disdainful of the doting swain Silvius, falls in love with Ganymede; Oliver, seeking his brother, repents when Orlando rescues him from a lioness; Rosalind is restored to her father; Duke Frederick arrives at Arden, has a religious conversion, and withdraws from the world (III.ii-V.iii).*

The two meetings of Rosalind and Orlando have always been seen as the comic heart of the play. They have the charm and vigour of the best romantic comedy, and they bring out the humour of others; e.g., the only tongues to be found in the trees are the rotten love poems Orlando places there. "Truly, the tree yields bad fruit," Touchstone wryly observes (III.ii.112). But Shakespeare intends that all of Nature should yield good fruit: the scenes echo the ancient wooing rituals — to produce fertility.

The first scene is unusual because Orlando exploits one of Rosalind's few failures of poise. Having learned from Celia that the verse hung "upon hawthornes" is his, Rosalind is distracted with nervous anticipation:

Alas the day, what shall I do with my doublet and hose?

What did he when thou sawest him? What said he? How

looked he? Wherein went he? What makes he here?
Did he ask for me? Where remains he? How parted he
with thee? And when shalt thou see him again? Answer
me in one word.   (III.ii.212-217)
Orlando enters, and this increases her girlish excitement. He
has already shown his "nimble wit": his parody of courtly manners as he leaves Jaques — "I do desire we may be better
strangers"; his defence of Rosalind — "There was no thought
of pleasing you when she was christened"; and when Jaques
invites him to join in railing against the world —

ORL: I will chide no breather in the world but myself,
      against whom I know most faults.
JAQ: The worst fault you have is to be in love.
ORL: 'Tis a fault I will not change for your best virtue.
                                                   (III.ii.272-275)
Orlando is an exceptional romantic hero. As Rosalind begins
to "speak to him like a saucy lackey," she blunders and asks
lamely, "I pray you, what is't o'clock?" Orlando's reply gives
unexpected point to the question. "You should ask me what
time o'day," he says. "There's no clock in the forest." Rosalind's
rejoinder that time is relative, travelling in "divers paces with
divers persons," is a brilliant recovery, but Orlando's insight is
equally shrewd (III.ii.291-300). Orlando is becoming her equal.

Their second encounter is delicious. In the theatre, players
discover that, where Rosalind had been the leader of the pair,
the question is now open. The scene relates closely to the sur-
rounding action. Their first meeting gains because it occurs
after the longest scene in the play. Then comes a scene of
Audrey and Touchstone. The scene between Silvius and Phebe
follows next. It precedes in turn the second meeting of
Rosalind and Orlando. Juxtapositions are important in *As You
Like It*, but once in the forest of Arden, the ideas contrasted are
not always those of court vs. country, or Fortune vs. Nature.
Now it is Ganymede vs. an emerging Orlando.

The plot is re-focused on the fortunes of the three pairs of
lovers midway in the play, so the poetic contrast of ideas shifts.
The stress is on love and wisdom (flexibility, natural life, seasonal time) vs. their negatives (rigidity, social life, clock time);
comic life vs. the denial of life. The profound truth discovered
by Rosalind and Orlando is their openness to multiple levels of

experience; they see different perspectives at the same time, and use several modes of experience without being locked into one. This truth is vastly different from the attitudes of the other couples: both the fleshly life of Touchstone and Audrey and the conventions of Silvius and Phebe are closed. For Rosalind, natural intuition is the key: "I will speak to him like a saucy lackey, and under that habit play the knave with him" — that is, she will do it because it "feels right." She and Orlando infuse life with a comic warmth which we can all share.

The finest moment in the play is the dazzling effect of a child actor playing Shakespeare's Rosalind, playing Rosalind's Ganymede, playing Ganymede's Rosalind. From experience with boy actors (Harehills, Leeds, 1952 and 1954), I can say it is even more extraordinary than in *Twelfth Night*. Rosalind's multiple roles create even more layers of irony. Although a man woos "a boy," there are no hints of homosexuality; despite her costume, we always know that Ganymede is physically Rosalind — even if played by a boy.

Rosalind's incredible virtuosity has obscured the fact that, in these scenes, Orlando is her imaginative equal. They are both players: they enter Arden disguised; his aggression at the forester's feast is a mask; when Ganymede plays "Rosalind," at times Orlando plays "Orlando" — his failure to dress in his role shows the separation of the two Orlandos (III.ii.357 ff.). Rosalind returns to it:

> ROS: ... if you break one jot of your promise, or come
> one minute behind your hour, I will think you
> the most pathetical break-promise, and the
> most hollow lover ... Therefore, beware my cen-
> sure, and keep your promise.   (IV.i.176-181)

Orlando's reply, "With no less religion than if thou wert indeed my Rosalind," is as ironic as anything spoken by Rosalind. Orlando initiates the end of the wooing of Ganymede: "I can live no longer by thinking" (V.ii.48) shows he is aware that Arden, like theatre, is a means to an end.

The Third Movement: The Wedding

The play ends with a quadruple wedding: Orlando-Rosalind, Oliver-Celia, Silvius-Phebe and Touchstone-

*Audrey. Duke Senior and his retinue (except for Jaques)
return to the court and prosperity (V.iv).*
The final scene has a fascinating depth of meaning. It is
directed by Rosalind who demonstrates the ancient power of
the female in two ways:

[1] As in the old Mother Goddess rituals (e.g., at
Eleusius), Rosalind brings about a ritual leading to the
fertility of the cosmos, the earth, and people.

[2] As in "the sacred marriage" rites (celebrated in the
great city of Sumer), Rosalind arranges the liminal
transition from courtship to marriage. This paradox
was fully accepted by the Elizabethans and by
Shakespeare: as the sun rules the heavens, and the
head rules the body, so the man is no longer the suitor
who serves, obeys, and begs. His role changes to the
husband who commands [See *End Notes*].

Rosalind explicitly submits to the two men in her life,
father and husband-to-be. She is straightforward and joyful as
to each she declares: "To you I give myself, for I am yours"
(lines 116-117). Thus she also submits to the patriarchal society
that they embody. Rosalind is not only a director: she plays the
role of a male possession. This should not offend feminists, as
she does so of her own free will. Within the Elizabethan context Rosalind's choice has charm: she is not forced to adopt
the role; her self-taming is voluntary, and its context differs
from Katherine's in *The Shrew*. Besides, Shakespeare the professional knows just how much change the Elizabethan audience
can take. When Rosalind gives herself to them both, she prevents potential hostility between her father and her fiancé; in
contrast to Cordelia, she ensures that each feels he has all her
love. Yet Rosalind does not really control this possible rivalry;
the male alliance of Duke Senior and Orlando was made at the
forest banquet.

Love and food are symbolically related. There is an unlimit-
ed supply of both — except for Jaques. He is the odd man out.
While all the other inhabitants of the forest of Arden who are
exiles from the court are only too ready to leave at the close,
Jaques is not.

The "happy ending" is a little odd, after all that has been
said about cuckoldry and April turning to December. Some

critics, surprisingly, cannot accept the four marriages as a happy ending when it includes Touchstone with his country wench Audrey: "A poor virgin, sir, an ill-favoured thing, sir, but mine own" (lines 56-57). But the fun and mockery have been directed mostly at pre-marital relations. Marriage, as part of a stable society, is not questioned. The gracious and stately Masque of Hymen (the urban god) marks the end of this interlude in the greenwood and announces the return to a court cleansed of envy. The last words about love, those that give it its proper place in an orderly society and prepare for the festive dance at the end, are delivered by Hymen:

> Wedding is great Juno's crown,
> O blessèd bond of board and bed;
> 'Tis Hymen peoples every town,
> High wedlock then be honourèd....   (138-141)

NATURE AND HUMAN NATURE

As You Like It takes place in an idyllic and naive world: the healthful greenwood, where men live in the simplicity of nature in harmony and innocence. The corrupt court is its contrast, and the balance between Fortune and Nature is the key to human happiness. As Rosalind tells Celia: "Fortune reigns in gifts of the world, not in the lineaments of Nature" (I.ii.40-41). Evil is in some men, goodness is in others: natural wickedness makes Oliver hate Orlando and Frederick banish Rosalind; and as his nature is noble, Duke Senior can find "good in everything." But Fortune is unjust: the nobler natures (Duke Senior, Rosalind, Celia, Orlando) suffer , but the wicked (Oliver, Frederick) thrive. All is resolved happily when the evil men are converted by contact with the good, while the good get the fortune their natures deserve. Shakespeare's other *play worlds* are more complex, and his people mix good with evil. But here human life is harmonious; good sense, love, humour, and a generous personality bring happiness.

Yet the play is not continuously idyllic. It is filled with sharp barbs, practical facts, and deep irony directed towards its chief themes: pastoral life and romantic love. For Shakespeare they are sentimental and foolish illusions. He laughs at them, opposes them, but finally lets them be. He reconciles the ideal with the actual — yet he avoids the uglier facts (this is noticed more by the reader than the audience).

Rosalind shows that the events of life are relative: "Time," she says, "travels in divers paces with divers persons" (III.ii.299-300). Time and life in the forest are understood differently by various people, and differently by one person according to who and where he or she is. Yet Rosalind's relativity is not exactly Einstein's. Touchstone, after he has arrived in Arden, is asked how he likes the shepherd's life and replies that a life spent apart from others appears to change its nature — to be relative to the person living it. Touchstone then asks Corin: "Hast any philosophy in thee, shepherd?" Corin responds: "No more but that I know the more one sickens, the worse at ease he is" (III.ii.21-23). It is not, as it might seem, that simple Corin has missed the point. Rather, his simplicity is wisdom: sickness is one of the things in life that is not psychologically relative; it is an absolute evil. The relativism of *As You Like It* is bounded by a set of moral absolutes.

LOVE

As life in the forest is not a fixed reality, love is potentially more complex. There is the romance of Rosalind and Orlando, the passion of Celia and Oliver, the matching of Silvius with Phebe, and the mating of Audrey with Touchstone. At first Silvius is the lovelorn shepherd of pastoral romance, and Phebe is his pouting shepherdess, but they become distasteful. Silvius' love is not combined with good sense. Phebe shows the response it will get from a petulant nature:

> But since that thou canst talk of love so well,
> Thy company, which erst was irksome to me,
> I will endure, and I'll employ thee too.
> But do not look for further recompense
> Than thine own gladness that thou art employed.
>
> (III.v.94-98)

Orlando and Rosalind show us romantic love as the best part of life so long as it is understood (as it is by Rosalind) to be only a part. Many romantic lines come from both of them which, if they were put together, would be sentimental. But there is always something sharp to taste. When Orlando swears that he will love her forever and a day, Rosalind says:

Say 'a day' without the 'ever.' No, no, Orlando, men
are April when they woo, December when they wed;
maids are May when they are maids, but the sky
changes when they are wives.   (IV.i.135-138)

She can even make bawdy jokes about love: in fact, Rosalind
runs the gamut of attitudes to love from romance to earthi-
ness.

Disillusioned remarks come chiefly from Jaques and
Touchstone. Jaques ridicules all human ideals, but his attacks
are not corrosive, and they are amusingly expressed. Those
who are most in love do not envy Jaques' detachment. Rosalind
says that those who are either too sad or too merry are "abom-
inable fellows," but between the two she would rather "have a
fool to make me merry than experience to make me sad"
(IV.i.25-26).

MALE AND FEMALE

The relation of men and women in *As You Like It* is highly complex. The idealized male society, centered on Duke Senior, is
founded on "sacred pity" and "kindness." It is very powerful.
Male bonds are superior to women's: men once separated are
reunited (Oliver, Orlando) but women united are separated by
marriage (Rosalind, Celia). Male power extends even to the
evil Oliver, threatened by a symbol of hostile female nurture:
"A lioness, with udders all drawn dry" and "the sucked and
hungry lioness." Orlando rescues his brother:

But kindness, nobler ever than revenge,
And nature, stronger than his just occasion,
Made him give battle to the lioness.
(IV.iii.115, 127, 129-131)

The tears "that sacred pity hath engendered" (II.vii.124) are
echoed in the brothers' reconciliation: "Tears our recount-
ments had most kindly bathed." Their reunion recapitulates
the banquet scene:

he led me to the gentle Duke,
Who gave me fresh array and entertainment,
Committing me unto my brother's love....
(IV.iii.141, 143-145)

Oliver says he wishes to marry Celia (V.ii.1-12) after he joins the male society. A pattern of male reconciliation preceding love for women emerges.

Rosalind wears the disguise of Ganymede, a male. As a supposed man she wields male powers and becomes the remarkable person that she is. The implications here are vital to an understanding of the play. Shakespeare's greatest female character in comedy becomes significant because she usurps maleness. And, moreover, she only returns to femininity because Shakespeare's society would not have it otherwise. Clearly he was trying to teach his contemporaries a very modern lesson.

Patriarchy is restored in the finale. As Rosalind's powers fade, the Duke announces Orlando's marriage inheritance: "A land itself at large, a potent dukedom" (V.iv.166). Ganymede then directs the men:

> ROS: You say, if I bring in your Rosalind, You will
> bestow her on Orlando here?
> DUKE: That would I, had I kingdoms to give with her.
> ROS: And you say you will have her, when I bring
> her?
> ORL.: That would I, were I of all kingdoms king.
>
> (V.iv.6-10)

Jaques de Boys brings the news of Duke Senior's restoration, and the re-uniting of the three de Boys sons establishes a continuity of generations.

In Arden, both men and women transcend typical gender roles: Rosalind gains male qualities through her costume, as Orlando gains female ones. But Rosalind's gain is only temporary. Orlando retains his gender but synthesizes male and female when he combines compassion-nurture and control-aggression to rescue his brother from the lioness. Whether male power is tyrannical or benevolent, it requires women to be subordinate, and Rosalind finally enacts this role. Festive celebration occurs because a male social order is secured. It is Duke Senior who legitimates the festive ritual:

> Play, music, and you brides and bridegrooms all,
> With measure heaped in joy, to th'measures fall.
>
> (V.iv.175-176)

As You Like It achieves a marital end not by eliminating male ties but rather by strengthening them.

In case we missed the message, Shakespeare decreases Rosalind's power again in the Epilogue when it is revealed that she is a boy actor:

> If I were a woman, I would kiss as many of you as had
> beards that pleased me....   (V.iv.211-212)

In the social structure of the play, male bonds provide political power. These bonds include heterosexual love because marriage incorporates women, but resistance to women remains. The Epilogue underlines Shakespeare's deep structure. This was necessary because Elizabethans (like all audiences) could confuse a light and airy surface structure with the deep and problematic issue which was as contemporary then as it is today.

ROSALIND

Although *As You Like It* is male-oriented, Rosalind is one of Shakespeare's most magnificent creations — perhaps the most exquisite, happy, and witty female role in all drama. With her blend of idealism and good sense, she becomes almost a symbol: she binds up wounds, reconciles estranged brothers, and unites lovers. Shakespeare explores all human nature through the myriad roles within the kaleidoscopic identity of a woman who is capable of being all things to all people.

The essence of Rosalind lies in her ability to view romance and sentiment from a truly comic perspective of joy and amusement. Rosalind sparkles with the vitality of Portia and the depth of Julia. Orlando tells Ganymede, in legalistic terms, he would die without Rosalind. She says:

> No, faith, die by attorney. The poor world is almost six
> thousand years old, and in all this time there was not
> any man died in his own person, *videlicet* [namely], in a
> love-cause ... men have died from time to time and
> worms have eaten them, but not for love.   (IV.i.85-98)

Her role-changing is the core of *As You Like It*. Rosalind accepts her dependent position at court. The superiority this gives her to Celia infuriates Frederick, and he banishes Rosalind for her merits:

> She is too subtle for thee, and her smoothness,
> Her very silence, and her patience
> Speak to the people, and they pity her.   (I.iii.75-77)

Celia bids her be merry despite her father's banishment, so she responds flippantly: "From henceforth I will, coz, and devise sports. Let me see — what think you of falling in love?" (I.ii.23-24). Love to her is a testing game as wrestling is for Orlando. Her surrender to love is more consciously explicit and candid than for any other Shakespearean heroine:

> He calls us back. My pride fell with my fortunes:
> I'll ask him what he would. — Did you call, sir?
> Sir, you have wrestled well, and overthrown
> More than your enemies.   (I.ii.241-244)

She is playing "the game" in earnest: the use of roles in courting was an essential part of Elizabethan courtly life.

The idea of the male disguise starts as a strategy for avoiding the normal female vulnerability to male sexual force:

> Alas, what danger will it be to us,
> Maids as we are, to travel forth so far?
> Beauty provoketh thieves sooner than gold.
>   (I.iii.106-108)

Ganymede's costume changes her identity: she can play both male and female roles, and analyzes her relationship to her various sexual roles by claiming many of the physical capacities of a man:

> Were it not better,
> Because that I am more than common tall,
> That I did suit me all points like a man?
> A gallant curtle-axe upon my thigh,
> A boar-spear in my hand, and in my heart
> Lie there what hidden woman's fear there will,
> We'll have a swashing and a martial outside,
> As many other mannish cowards have
> That do outface it with their semblances. (I.iii.112-120)

For us, her femininity often shows through the mask of Ganymede. She deplores Phebe's abuse of Silvius because it discredits her sex. Celia teases her by holding back the news that Orlando is in the forest, and Rosalind explodes in impatience: "Dost thou think, though I am caparisoned [dressed] like a man, I have a doublet and hose in my disposition?" (III.ii.188-190). Oliver produces a handkerchief stained with Orlando's blood (he has been slightly wounded by the lioness), and Ganymede swoons, which she claims was "counterfeited."

Oliver says let Ganymede counterfeit to be a man. She replies: "So I do; but, i'faith, I should have been a woman by right" (IV.iii.174-175).

She excels in her scenes as Ganymede with Orlando. Some foolish lover, says Ganymede, is ruining the forest, carving "Rosalind" on the barks of trees. But it could not be Orlando: he does not have the proper symptoms —

> A lean cheek, which you have not; a blue [dark circles under the] eye and sunken, which you have not; an unquestionable [silent] spirit, which you have not; a beard neglected, which you have not ... Then your hose should be ungartered, your bonnet unbanded, your sleeve unbuttoned, your shoe untied, and everything about you demonstrating a careless desolation.
>
> (III.ii.358-366)

When Orlando is late for his appointment, Ganymede rails:

> Break an hour's promise in love? He that will divide a minute into a thousand parts, and break but a part of the thousandth part of a minute in the affairs of love, it may be said of him that Cupid hath clapped him o'th' shoulder, but I'll warrant him heart-whole.   (IV.i.39-43)

She dissolves into a young woman in love, then returns to "the game":

> ROS: Come, woo me, woo me: for now I am in a holi-
>   day humour, and like enough to consent. What
>   would you say to me now, an I were your very,
>   very Rosalind?
>
> ORL: I would kiss before I spoke.
>
> ROS: Nay, you were better speak first, and when you
>   were gravelled [stuck] for lack of matter, you
>   might take occasion to kiss. Very good orators,
>   when they are out, they will spit, and for lovers
>   lacking — God warn us! — matter, the cleanli-
>   est shift is to kiss.   (IV.i.61-70)

She can barely wait to tell Celia of her ecstasy:

> O coz, coz, coz, my pretty little coz, that thou didst
> know how many fathom deep I am in love! But it can-
> not be sounded: my affection hath an unknown bot-
> tom, like the Bay of Portugal... I'll tell thee, Aliena, I
> cannot be out of the sight of Orlando: I'll go find a
> shadow and sigh till he come.   (IV.i.190-202)

Though she teases Orlando with the wife's power by using her "wayward wit" (IV.i.154-177), this is simply good fun. The audience understands that Rosalind's role as disloyal wife is a fiction, not a genuine threat; we know that, once married, she will be faithful. She is concerned not with her loyalty but Orlando's, as her sudden change of tone when he announces his departure shows: "Alas, dear love, I cannot lack thee two hours!" (IV.i.165). She fears his betrayal: "Ay, go your ways, go your ways: I knew what you would prove" (IV.i.168-169). Rosalind is vulnerable despite her wit. She anxiously waits for him: "But why did he swear he would come this morning, and comes not?" (III.iv.17-18). Her own behaviour neutralizes her jokes about cuckoldry, and this neutrality is reinforced by the brief account of the male hunt: the expected negative meaning of horns as "cuckold" is transformed into a positive image of phallic potency that unites men. Yet Rosalind is unquestionably in love, as she confesses to Celia in her "coz, coz, coz" speech. Her disguise allows her to express many unromantic sentiments, but they are Rosalind's as much as Ganymede's. While in love she realizes what love may become, and how it can appear to those who are not in love.

Shakespeare brilliantly shows Rosalind's emotional growth to womanhood: from her initial unawakened state, through sexual excitement, to wry self-awareness, and to her reconciliation in marriage. Apart from Jaques, only she knowingly develops her own nature by choice. Once in the forest, her attitudes to her own nature oscillate: she can ask, "Do you not know I am a woman? When I think, I must speak" (III.ii.242-243), and she can assert to Orlando, "Me believe it? You may as soon make her that you love believe it, which I warrant she is apter to do than to confess she does" (III.ii.371-373). As she pretends to flirt maliciously with Orlando, Rosalind enjoys a harmless delight in teasing; yet she also recognizes this as frivolous, if not contemptible. She progresses from flirtation to a serious rehearsal of the marriage ceremony, commenting, "There's a girl goes before the priest, and certainly a woman's thought runs before her actions" (IV.i.128-130). She prepares for a role she will soon adopt in earnest, but not at the expense of her liveliness — "The wiser, the waywarder" (IV.i.150).

Rosalind's sexual experience anticipates our own times. The "doubling" of her sexual identity makes Rosalind intriguing to modern audiences accustomed to androgyny. We enjoy Rosalind's dazzling sexual finesse and the virtuosity with which she complicates her sexual roles. Rosalind experiments most successfully with the range of love relationships open to both sexes, responding creatively to the nuances of romantic feeling and action. Her sexual insights are so potent that she anticipates Prospero: "Believe then ... that I can do strange things ... and yet not damnable ... though I say I am a magician" (V.ii.56-68).

She solves the emotional tangles around her without false rhetoric or drastic action. She presents herself as what she *should* be, so the problems evaporate. Rosalind is what each woman hopes to be: emotionally committed to femininity yet sexually experienced in both male and female attitudes and both witty and sceptical enough never to be caught in an unwanted role. She does not integrate gender differences: her insistence on the metaphor of exterior (male) and interior (female) keeps them distinct. And her liberation does not last; as the play returns to the normal world, she is reduced to the traditional woman, subservient to men.

The performer of Rosalind must integrate the actual and fictional worlds. Although she must feel that love is a good time of life, it is not everything. But in its season it would be stupid not to enjoy it — which the performer must convey to the audience.

ORLANDO

Orlando is as difficult a role as Rosalind but for very different reasons. He has been criticized as unworthy of Rosalind, but this is far from the case. He begins as a violent and aggressive young man, brawling and wrestling, and even Rosalind is surprised that she falls in love with him: "Pray heaven I be deceived in you," she says to Orlando. She is, indeed, because he grows even more than she does. He overcomes his earlier failings and becomes a match for her, not only in wit but also in sensitivity, awareness and control.

This is not always obvious to the reader (though it is to the audience) because of Orlando's position in two kinds of scenes in the forest. First, while Rosalind's confidante Celia gives her the opportunity to talk about love, Orlando is accompanied by Adam, who serves a very different function. He is a living link to Orlando's father: the paternal inheritance blocked by Oliver is received indirectly by Orlando from Adam when he offers Orlando money:

> I saved under your father,
> Which I did store to be my foster-nurse.... (II.iii.39-40)

Second, in the Ganymede scenes the plot ensures that Rosalind leads Orlando. But in the playing, these scenes reveal Orlando undergoing continuous growth. He is purged of a lover's sentimental affectations by brilliant instruction in female unpredictability. In another paradox, he comes to know the nature of his mistress fully only because, for a time at least, he fails to recognize her. Orlando proves that he is the right husband for Rosalind and shows himself gentle, courteous, generous and brave, and a match for her in wit.

THE TWO COMMENTATORS

The play is unique in having two commentators: Touchstone the parodist and Jaques the cynic. Touchstone enjoys life but parodies it. He fits clowning to everyone, using many roles: after Silvius's lament, he is the maudlin lover of Jane Smile; for the simple shepherd Corin he is the worldly-wise courtier; with Jaques he is a melancholy moralist; and with the pages he is the patron of the arts. Jaques is his opposite. As a cynic he prefers to be superior, apart from ordinary life. Villains can be converted, but he cannot. He will not swim in the water but prefers to "fish for fancies as they pass."

Touchstone often puts Jaques in his place. Jaques boasts that he met a fool in the forest, not realizing the fool was mocking him. "It is ten o'clock," Touchstone says seriously:

> 'Thus we may see,' quoth he, 'how the world wags:
> 'Tis but an hour ago since it was nine,
> And after one hour more 'twill be eleven,
> And so from hour to hour, we ripe, and ripe,
> And then from hour to hour, we rot and rot,
> And thereby hangs a tale.' (II.vii.23-28)

Here Touchstone mocks the "seven ages" speech, but his explicit parody of Jaques's hollow rhetoric is his lecture on the seven degrees of quarreling: Retort Courteous, Quip Modest, Reply Churlish, Reproof Valiant, Countercheck Quarrelsome, Lie Circumstantial, and the Lie Direct (V.iv.70-94).

Touchstone and Jaques are alike in their rejection of the ideal and, therefore, in their incompleteness. For them the ideal is absurd.

JAQUES

Jaques is Shakespeare's version of a stage figure familiar in his day, the *malcontent*. First found in the bitter verse satires of John Marston in the 1590s, from 1599 he appears in plays, defending his snarling attacks and abusive words as the only way to purge the world of vice. The good Duke attacks Jaques as if he were such a type, and he replies in the usual way (II.vii), but Shakespeare has changed the type. Jaques tries to cleanse "the foul body of th'infected world" (II.vii.60), and, like others in Arden, he says he loathes the court, but everything does not disgust him. He enjoys Amien's bittersweet songs ("Under the Greenwood Tree" and "Blow, Blow, Thou Winter Wind"): "I can suck melancholy out of a song as a weasel sucks eggs. More, I prithee, more" (II.v.11-13). The Duke treats him like a court entertainer, and he is a natural butt for Orlando and Rosalind.

Jaques has a sour distaste for life; without him, we might find life in Arden too sweet. His only action is to interfere in the marriage of Touchstone and Audrey, and this he only postpones. The others enjoy his company. Duke Senior loves to be with him in his "sullen fits," when Jaques is "full of matter," and he urges Jaques to return with him to the court. Jaques claims his malady comes from extensive travel and experience:

> JAQ: I have neither the scholar's melancholy, which
> is emulation; nor the musician's, which is fan-
> tastical; nor the courtier's, which is proud; nor
> the soldier's, which is ambitious; nor the
> lawyer's, which is politic; nor the lady's, which is
> nice; nor the lover's, which is all these: but it is
> a melancholy of mine own, compounded of

many simples, extracted from many objects,
and indeed the sundry contemplation of my
travels, in which my often rumination wraps me
in a most humorous sadness.

ROS: Farewell, Monsieur Traveller. Look you lisp and
wear strange suits; disable all the benefits of
your own country; be out of love with your
nativity, and almost chide God for making you
that countenance you are; or I will scarce think
you have swam in a gondola. (IV.i.10-18, 29-34)

To Jaques, nothing has purpose or value. His most famous
speech is, quite properly from him, a detached chronicle of
man's futility:

All the world's a stage,
And all the men and women merely players;
They have their exits and their entrances,
And one man in his time plays many parts,
His Acts being seven ages. (II.vii.140-144)

This speech has many functions. It shows Jaques' character,
and it is a key to the play's design. It is also the most fully for-
mulated example of the play metaphor ubiquitous in Shakespeare. Jaques' speech is preceded and inspired by Duke
Senior's realization that "we are not alone unhappy":

This wide and universal theatre
Presents more woeful pageants than the scene
Wherein we play in. (II.vii.138-140)

For Jaques, a role is recognizable from its familiarity, the con-
ventionality of its gestures and moves, in which he finds sharp
humour:

Then, the whining schoolboy, with his satchel
And shining morning face, creeping like snail
Unwillingly to school; and then the lover,
Sighing like furnace, with a woeful ballad
Made to his mistress' eyebrow.... (II.vii.146-150)

Far from bitter, it shows that Jaques is another brilliant performer; in the role of brooding cynic he hides a genial interest
in humanity.

Shakespeare uses "All the world's a stage" to develop Arden
as a theatre, a key to the contrast between forest and court. It is
a stage for many brief playlets: Rosalind tells Celia, "I will speak

to [Orlando] like a saucy lackey, and under that habit play the knave with him" (III.ii.287-288); Corin, finding Silvius wooing Phebe, invites the others to "see a pageant truly played," and Rosalind promises to "prove a busy actor in their play" (III.iv.47, 54). Many playlets explore the illusions of lovers: the conventional stereotype in Ganymede's account of its essential "marks" (III.ii.358-366); love romantic — Rosalind-Orlando, Celia-Oliver — and pastoral — Phebe-Silvius, Phebe-Ganymede; a parody of these in Touchstone's marrying the "foul slut," Audrey, to avoid living "in bawdry" (III.iii.33, 87); and Jaques's rejection of love (III.ii.246-286).

Jaques is "the outsider": a solitary figure who does nothing to harm anyone. In the final pairings, he is the one left out. "I am for other than for dancing measures," says Jaques. Leaving the hateful sight of revelling, he goes to the house of penitents, where he joins Frederick as "There is much matter to be heard and learned" (V.iv.182).

It is characteristic of Shakespeare's comedies to include an element that is irreconcilable, which strikes a lightly discordant note: in *Love's Labour's Lost* he dared to allow the news of a death to cloud the revels at the close; in *The Merchant* and *Much Ado*, he asks us to accept that some people are positively wicked; and at the end of *Twelfth Night*, the impotent misery and fury of the humiliated Malvolio's last words, "I'll be revenged on the whole pack of you," call in question comedy itself. Jaques has the same position in *As You Like It* but with much less emphasis.

TOUCHSTONE

Touchstone differs from Shakespeare's earlier clowns. This may be the result of a personnel change in the Lord Chamberlain's Men, namely, the departure of Will Kempe in 1599 and the arrival of Robert Armin. Kempe's was a broad humour (Bottom, Dogberry), but Armin's talent lay chiefly in witty repartée. In *As You Like It* the emphasis shifts in the same way, with Touchstone the first in a line of court jesters that includes Feste in *Twelfth Night* and the poignant Fool in *King Lear.* Touchstone's wit is of the detached kind, quick to see the folly and absurdity of life. "He uses his folly like a stalking-horse," Duke Senior says of him, "and under the presentation of that he shoots his wit" (V.iv.103-104).

Whatever the idealized life in court or country, for Touchstone there is little to choose between them. When Corin asks how he likes the shepherd's life, Touchstone replies:

> Truly, shepherd, in respect of itself, it is a good life; but in respect that it is a shepherd's life, it is naught. In respect that it is solitary, I like it very well; but in respect that it is private, it is a very vile life. Now in respect it is in the fields, it pleaseth me well; but in respect it is not in the court, it is tedious. As it is a spare life, look you, it fits my humour well; but as there is no more plenty in it, it goes much against my stomach.
>
> (III.ii.13-20)

Like the wise fool that he is, Touchstone alters his manner to fit the quality and the mood of the persons with whom he jests. With his mistress and Rosalind, he is properly subservient except for the odd impertinence that breaks through. His gross parody of Orlando's lyrics is mostly amusing and apt, but it gets increasingly more outspoken in its sexuality:

> If a hart do lack a hind,
> Let him seek out Rosalind.
> If the cat will after kind,
> So be sure will Rosalind...
> Sweetest nut hath sourest rind,
> Such a nut is Rosalind.
> He that sweetest rose will find,
> Must find love's prick and Rosalind.   (III.ii.97-108)

Any woman would resent verse that likens her to a hind and a cat in heat. Touchstone is usually less crude and direct, softened by self-mockery. But he is the ideal fool for Rosalind. Early in the play, she hails him as "Nature's natural the cutter-off of Nature's wit," and Celia says, "always the dullness of the fool is the whetstone of the wits" (I.ii.47, 52). He enjoys the vigorous give-and-take of debate, which he almost always wins. After Rosalind has called him a dull fool and has sharpened her wit upon him, Touchstone answers simply, "You have said; but whether wisely or no, let the forest judge" (III.ii.117). Rosalind says, "Thou speakest wiser than thou art ware of" (II.iv.52), and the fool agrees with her. Jaques says, "He's as good at anything, and yet a fool." Touchstone agrees when Jaques introduces him as "the motley-minded gentleman" (V.iv.101, 40). He not only accepts his role but revels in it, which distinguishes Touchstone from less wise fools. In meeting Jaques, Touchstone observes the courtesies while patronizing Jaques who has condescended to him:

> Good even, good Master What-ye-call't: how do you,
> sir? You are very well met. God 'ild [God reward] you
> for your last company, I am very glad to see you. Even a
> toy in hand here, sir. Nay, pray be covered.
>
> (III.iii.67-70)

Touchstone parodies courtly manners, just as he later makes fun of the etiquette of the duello. To the Duke, Touchstone is properly courteous. There is genuine humility in his reply to the Duke's praise:

> DUKE: By my faith, he is very swift and sententious.
> TOUCH: According to the fool's bolt, sir, and such
>   dulcet diseases.   (V.iv.61-63)

His use of the old proverb, "a fool's bolt is soon shot," shows he does not take himself too seriously. It is different when he meets the rustics:

> COR: You have too courtly a wit for me; I'll rest.
> TOUCH: Wilt thou rest damned? God help thee,
>   shallow man! God make incision in thee,
>   thou art raw!   (III.ii.66-68)

In saluting the clown William, he is more condescending than in his greeting of Jaques:

> TOUCH: Good even, gentle friend. Cover thy head,
>   cover thy head; nay, prithee, be covered. How
>   old are you, friend?
> WILL: Five-and-twenty, sir.
> TOUCH: A ripe age. Is thy name William?
> WILL: William, sir.
> TOUCH: A fair name. Wast born i'th'forest here?
> WILL: Ay, sir, I thank God.
> TOUCH: 'Thank God:' a good answer.   (V.i.16-24)

Suddenly abandoning his friendly tone toward the lout, Touchstone bursts into a torrent of turgid and unprovoked abuse:

I will deal in poison with thee, or in bastinado, or in
steel; I will bandy with thee in faction; I will o'er-run
thee with policy; I will kill thee a hundred and fifty ways
— therefore tremble and depart.   (V.i.53-56)
His bluster, of course, is not serious, and the storm dies as
quickly as it arises. It is not to so much directed at poor William
as it is at "poetasters" like Marston who use this sort of bombast
in all seriousness.

Touchstone's marriage to Audrey, the simple-minded
goatherd, is itself a parody (Shakespeare's more than
Touchstone's) on romance and pastoralism; but it is also a
comment on the limitations of Touchstone's view of life. The
play borders on the grotesque in Touchstone's wooing of
Audrey: "Well, praised be the gods for thy foulness; sluttishness
may come hereafter" (III.iii.36-37). This is not cynicism, for
Touchstone is a genial humorist. He also shows a wholesome
regard for the realities of marriage: "As the ox has his bow, sir,
the horse his curb, and the falcon her bells, so man hath his
desires; and as pigeons bill, so wedlock would be nibbling"
(III.iii.72-74). Touchstone is a realist who believes that happiness derives from bodily satisfactions.

"ALL THE WORLD'S A STAGE"

When Shakespeare uses "All the world's a stage" to develop
Arden as a theatre, he contrasts the idyllic world to life at
court. The fictional world reveals the truth about the actual
world — just as the world of the playhouse reveals Elizabethans
to themselves. We discover truth through fiction. Rosalind, for
example, integrates the actual and fictional worlds when
Ganymede becomes her role.

Fiction contrasts with fact — but they are not opposites. The
actual and fictional are similars with differences. Actual life and
fictional life are so much alike they are homologous. One is the
mirror of the other, and, by a comparison of one with another,
truth is revealed. The "truths" discovered in the play include:
fertility is the aim of life; life is relative but is bounded by a set
of moral absolutes; evil men are converted by contact with good
sense, love, humour, and a generous personality; and human

beings strive to recognize and use the multiple levels of experience. Shakespeare leaves many other issues unresolved.

The relation of life to the stage is built on the dialogue of human interaction. For Shakespeare, in life we are "merely players": two subjectivities who meet and create a dialogue — a double structure. Roles are the media in which we create meaning, and our understanding reveals truth. Rosalind and Orlando know what love is through the medium of Ganymede, a fictional role. Actual-fictional, life-theatre, Rosalind-Ganymede, face-mask, person-role, male-female, truth-fiction, forest-court, love-sex, youth-age, etc. — each is a double structure: a metaphor of similars revealing difference. Symbolically this structure is expressed as Power vs. Love, which changes its emphasis as the play proceeds. In the First Movement it focuses on the wrestling match as discord: servitude vs. freedom, Oliver vs. Orlando, Frederick vs. Rosalind. But in the forest, the structure shifts to love and wisdom vs. their negatives; comic life vs. the denial of life.

At a deep level this becomes male-female: how can women in society control their lives? Shakespeare establishes a male caring society which is based on "sacred pity," "kindness," and non-violence. In the restorative greenwood, men live in the simplicity of nature in harmony and innocence. Symbolically implicit here, Love = Food becomes explicit at the weddings.

In Arden, both men and women transcend typical gender roles: Rosalind gains male qualities through disguise, as Orlando gains female ones. On the stage, Rosalind is a living metaphor, an image that exemplifies the play: a boy playing Rosalind playing Ganymede playing Rosalind. The metaphor is rich in sexual ambiguity. What is reality? Rosalind in the clothing of Ganymede (androgyny — one level of illusion) challenges the male world of Duke Senior (Christianity — a second level of illusion).

The relation of the male-oriented society to Christianity is clear. The number of religious references in *As You Like It* has often been commented on. Many are of little significance. But some are explicit and have a serious, unforced beauty: e.g., Orlando's appeal to outlawed men,

If ever you have looked on better days;
If ever been where bells have knolled to church ...
(II.vii.114-115)
Adam's prayer,
... He that doth the ravens feed,
Yea, providently caters for the sparrow, .
Be comfort to my age ...   (II.iii.43-45)
and Corin's recognition, from St. Paul, that we have to find the
way to heaven by doing deeds of hospitality (II.iv.78-79).

Yet the god of marriage, Hymen, speaks solemnly. His
opening words with their New Testament echo are conventional:
Then is there mirth in heaven,
When earthly things, made even,
Atone together.   (V.iv.105-107)
Rosalind organizes a ritual marriage whereby women surrender
power to men. But the appearance of the god to present
daughter to father, and to bless the brides and grooms, turns
the end of the play into a solemn occasion in four ways:

- it formalizes what is already a very ritualistic play;
- it provides an image of the concord which reigns in
  Heaven and which Heaven blesses on earth;
- it unifies the play with the world of Queen Elizabeth I, in
  which allegorical pageantry occurs everywhere; and
- it concludes the action with a graceful spectacle.

At one level the play is a simple pastoral tale. At another, it
raises major metaphysical and social issues. In Shakespeare's
terms, you may take it *As You Like It.*

TWELFTH NIGHT

WITH HEY, HO, THE WIND AND THE RAIN

Of the three great romantic comedies Shakespeare wrote around the year 1600, *Twelfth Night* is the last and most fragile. Consequently it can be performed in a wide variety of ways: broadly, prettily, sadly or, as Sir Tyrone Guthrie directed it, almost as a "dark" comedy. With its many possible interpretations, it contrasts sharply with the brittle dialogue of *Much Ado* and the festivity of *As You Like It*. It is Shakespeare's last pure comedy, and as we never quite know what we shall see when we enter the theatre, it is his most magical because it is always fresh.

Samuel Johnson missed the point when he said that *Twelfth Night* fails the test of relevance. Superficially, it is like most romantic comedies: coincidence exposes folly and rewards virtue; the plot has a shipwreck, a journey to a distant land, noble lovers and a maiden in distress; there are disguises and mistaken identities, and a pretentious ass is put down by merrymakers. There is deathless poetry, an effortless construction, music throughout and some lovely songs. Critics cannot be blamed for thinking that, in this play, form and style are all.

But *Twelfth Night* is also directly relevant to our lives. Like the plays of Sophocles and Pirandello, it asks who am I, and who am I for other people? Primarily, *Twelfth Night* is *a study in self-deception:* it shows the difficulty people have in knowing themselves. Shakespeare asks the same questions many times, for example when Richard II, stripped of his crown, explores his final recognition of himself, and when Lear tears off his clothing to reveal the elemental man. For Shakespeare, to show a person's growth toward self-awareness is what plays are all about.

This massive theme has a universal application, but it receives its consummate comic statement in *Twelfth Night.* Shakespeare re-creates it not only in romantic comedy but also for a specific audience. He does so with most of his comedies, but in *Twelfth Night* love is delayed not by traditional factors, like parental disapproval, but by people's own deceits and self-deceptions. To Shakespeare most people are trapped by their illusions as if they are, as Pirandello would say, "fixed" like a moth pinned to a collector's board. Most are victims of their own folly.

HISTORY OF THE PLAY

The sole source for the text is the Folio (1623), which presents few problems. The earliest recorded performance was at the Middle Temple, on February 2, 1602, before an audience of law students. It followed close on *As You Like It,* and there are clues pointing to earlier performances: in 1600, or the autumn of 1599, under the title of *What You Will* (linking it with *As You Like It* and *Much Ado*); and at court before the Queen on Twelfth Night, 1600. The title seems derived from its performance on that day.

An alternative view of the play's origins is given by Leslie Hotson in *The First Night of Twelfth Night.** Although many scholars disagree with him, Hotson believes that the first performance was at Court on Epiphany (Twelfth Night), 6 January 1601 at the Noon Hall in Whitehall Palace. On that day, Elizabeth entertained Don Virginio Orsino, Duke of Bracciano, and a Russian ambassador.

Olivia represents the Queen, Orsino is the Italian visitor, and Malvolio is a caricature of Sir William Knollys, Controller of the Queen's Household. Knollys disliked revels and was known as "old Party Beard" for dyeing his beard. He was ripe for satire because he lusted after his young ward, "Mall" Fitton. Shakespeare exposed him in the name *Mala-voglia* (Ill Will, or Evil Concupiscence), or perhaps *Mal-voglio* ("I want Mall").

---

* Hotson (1961).

The forged letter asks Malvolio to appear before Olivia in yellow stockings and cross-garters, but, like Olivia, Queen Elizabeth abhorred yellow. Hotson thinks that the play was presented "in the round," which might make sense of Illyria's dramatic space.

The adventures of identical twins are as old as European literature. The twins had different sexes in the anonymous Sienese comedy, *Gl'Ingannati* ("The Deceived Ones"), first performed in 1531; and Shakespeare was generally indebted to the *commedia dell'arte*. He probably knew of John Lyly's *Gallathea,* in which a girl is disguised as a boy, acted before 1588. But the main plot of *Twelfth Night* comes directly from Barnabe Riche's story of Apolonius and Silla (1581).

Samuel Pepys in the 1600s characterized *Twelfth Night* as a "silly play." Its modern history began when Charles Macklin played Malvolio (1741); since then the play has never been long absent from the London stage.* Charles Lamb first thought that Malvolio might be tragic, but this was not the only view: Samuel Phelps in 1848 was comically self-satisfied, neither asking for pity nor evoking it; but in 1857 he played the role again with Spanish gravity and was less comic and more sympathetic. Henry Irving's tragic Malvolio (1884), based on Lamb's essay, influenced far more than his own generation. Harley Granville-Barker established *Twelfth Night* as a classic (1912): he rejected elaborate scenery, returned to the original order of the scenes, and allowed one scene to flow into another; he also restrained the physical action, especially the clowning of Sir Andrew and Sir Toby. Three modern productions by the Royal Shakespeare Company have had considerable influence: Peter Hall's "Chekhovian" version (1958), John Barton's "bare" production, with Donald Sinden as a comic and heroic Malvolio (1969-1972), and John Caird's very sad version (1983). My two productions were very different from each other. At Leeds (Harehills School, 1950) I cast boys as girls on a temporary Elizabethan stage, but with the Huddersfield Thespians (1956) I cast women and used a proscenium stage. The second had a

---

* For theatre history see Barnet (1965), Granville-Barker (1912), Salgado (1975), Sprague (1944, 1953), and Sprague and Trewin (1970).

twenty minutes' longer running-time than the first (using an identical script) and, despite the depth of character achieved by the Huddersfield adults, the Leeds production better captured the innate nature of the play.

ROLES, PLOT AND STRUCTURE

Shakespeare's structural abilities are extraordinary as he alters his frameworks from play to play, adjusting to his material. Nowhere is this better seen than in *Twelfth Night*. He begins the linear structure simply enough. The First Movement consists of scenes which establish the context of the play: first, the main localities of Illyria: two great houses and the exterior; and second the data necessary to begin the two plots: the persons and circumstances of the Duke, Olivia, Viola, and the revellers. The plot which develops in the Second Movement has three main lines of action: Orsino's languid courtship of Olivia, Olivia's confusion between Viola and Sebastian, and Malvolio's disgrace. But in an extraordinary way, they appear not as isolated actions but as reciprocal parts of one situation (the gulling of Malvolio). In *Twelfth Night* Shakespeare achieves his greatest unity of plot. It is as though he starts with all the play in his mind and simply lets it flow as a spontaneous creative process. When he ties the ends up in the Third Movement, this spontaneity provides him with some small difficulties, but the play continues as a wonderful creation to the end.

The epilogue of Feste's song is an inherent part of the play's structure, but it gives the whole a unique frame. The play has just ended happily when the Clown steps forward and sings a strange mixture of seriousness and nonsense. Feste, in words that mysteriously seem to recall St. Paul's "When I was a child" [1 Cor. 13: 11], reminds the audience that the play is done:

> When that I was and a little tiny boy,
> With hey, ho, the wind and the rain —
> A foolish thing was but a toy,
> For the rain it raineth every day.   (V.i.386-389)

On one level Feste presents a jaunty and obscene history of love and its trials. But the song also has the bittersweet quality of a harsh world beyond the play. Illyria seems a shade more melancholy, and more fragile, than it did within the *play world*.

This atmosphere has led some critics, and not a few stage directors, to see the play itself as darker than it really is; they have judged the action from the view of the epilogue. The play's structure reveals the continuous dramatic action of the bare Elizabethan stage. The arrangements of events is swift, clean and simple. The locality changes constantly, and, by ignoring the Folio's non-Shakespearean instructions, we see that in most cases it is unspecified. The time of the play's action is any time that suits the plot. Scenery is unnecessary apart from one tree for the garden scene. And, at best, the whole takes place without a break. The three-dimensional Elizabethan stage fits the Shakespearean complexity, enabling the dramatist to juxtapose contrasted characters, so that (say) Malvolio is on one side, and the eavesdroppers are on the other, binding together soliloquy and aside.

If the linear structure is in three Movements, the poetic (spatial) structure is founded on roles and disguise. Shakespeare first uses the device of disguise in *Two Gentlemen* but repeats it with variations in every other comedy. Like Rosalind, Viola is dressed as a girl to begin with but becomes a boy for the rest of the play. She is a very different youth from Rosalind; the whole charm of the part is the gentle girlhood that breathes behind the male doublet. The Viola-Orsino and Viola-Olivia interactions, the subtlest and loveliest scenes in the play, depend entirely upon the disguise. Their emotional quality is exquisite and provides a perfect blend of tenderness, beauty and true comedy. The whole idea of disguise and roles becomes the controlling metaphor of the play.

ACTION

The First Movement: The Context

The essence of *Twelfth Night* is given to us here: the coast and two great houses in romantic Illyria; the basis of the main plot (Orsino's and Olivia's emotional indulgence and Viola's strength and gentleness in love); and the sub-plot within Olivia's household. Shakespeare is now at the peak of his comic powers, and, with astounding economy, in three short scenes of contrasting pace (languorous, brisk, and rollicking) he allows us to experience each element as virtually one whole within a comic play world.

> *At his palace, Duke Orsino of Illyria bids his musicians play to soothe his love-melancholy for Olivia. She will live in seclusion for seven years to mourn her brother (I.i).*
> If music be the food of love, play on,
> Give me excess of it, that, surfeiting,
> The appetite may sicken, and so die.
> That strain again! It had a dying fall.
> O, it came o'er my ear like the sweet sound
> That breathes upon a bank of violets,
> Stealing and giving odour. Enough, no more!
> 'Tis not so sweet now as it was before. (1-8)

This famous opening achieves many effects. We grasp the core of the main plot: Orsino languishes for the Countess Olivia who, in mourning, has abjured the company of men for seven years. Like the Forest of Arden, Illyria is for lovers but in a very different way: the prevailing comic mood is one of sentiment, sadness, and not a little sentimentality. With twice as many songs as *As You Like It*, music saturates the play.* Music constantly accompanies Orsino. There is also all the music of Shakespeare's verse, here at its sweetest: the glorious poetry lies on the cusp between his comedies and his tragedies.

"If music be the food of love ..." That this is one of Shakespeare's loveliest openings is no reason for its meaning to be hidden. It gives us all we need to know about Orsino. The Duke's lush poetry establishes a crucial theme: *self-discovery through excess* — by a surfeit of feasting, physical or emotional, "the appetite may sicken, and so die." People discover their false roles and, thus, the truth about themselves. Love is a tyranny: it accepts all offerings but makes them seem worthless:

> O spirit of love, how quick and fresh art thou,
> That, notwithstanding thy capacity
> Receiveth as the sea, naught enters there,

---

* *Twelfth Night* ends with "When that I was and a little tiny boy" (V.i.386), and the play has two of Shakespeare's loveliest songs: "O, mistress mine" (II.iii.37ff.) and "Come away, come away death" (II.iv.50ff).

> Of what validity and pitch soe'er,
> But falls into abatement and low price
> Even in a minute.   (9-14)

Love disregards even the lover: when first Orsino saw Olivia,

> That instant was I turned into a hart,
> And my desires, like fell and cruel hounds,
> E'er since pursue me.   (22-24)

Orsino must keep feeding love with one satisfaction after another. That is, Orsino is making an excuse for emotional self-indulgence: he wants it to continue; he does not want to satisfy it. To him, Olivia is a means, not an end: she is not an object to be attained but a stimulant; she intoxicates the yearning and melancholy in which he delights. He enjoys his pain: he is in love with love. Olivia has similar problems. She has some cause — she has lost her father and brother within a twelvemonth — but she too feeds on her sorrow:

> The element itself, till seven years' heat,
> Shall not behold her face at ample view,
> But like a cloistress she will veilèd walk,
> And water once a day her chamber round
> With eye-offending brine; all this to season
> A brother's dead love, which she would keep fresh
> And lasting, in her sad remembrance. ·   (27-33)

Orsino admires this love for her brother, even as he complains of her cruelty to him. Everyone in Illyria lacks a sense of proportion. Orsino wallows in his love as Olivia does in her grief. Both are self-centered, caught up in their emotions: she in her mourning, he in his loving. When love's appetite for this or that dies, Orsino must turn to something else.

> Away before me to sweet beds of flowers!
> Love thoughts lie rich when canopied with bowers.
>   (41-42)

Viola, shipwrecked and presuming her twin brother Sebastian dead, arrives on the coast of Illyria. She persuades the sea captain to present her to Orsino as a boy page (I.ii).

VIOLA: My brother, he is in Elysium.
           Perchance he is not drowned. What think
           you, sailors?

CAPTAIN: It is perchance that you yourself were saved.
VIOLA: O, my poor brother! and so perchance may
            he be.   (4-7)

There is a sharp change of tempo and mood with Viola's
opening lines. She is brisk like her twin, with a sense of proportion about something as painful as the loss of her brother. Apart
from the twins, almost all the others in the play are shackled, in
varying degrees, by their inability to comprehend their own
emotions or even to see their blunders. We know Viola at once:
she is open, honest, confident, charming, and wealthy. She
should go to her father's friend for protection. But hearing
Orsino's name she says, "He was a bachelor then." She wants to
see if she wishes to woo him, which she cannot do if she appears
as a woman, for Orsino would have to send her home. So she
bribes the captain:

I prithee — and I'll pay thee bounteously —
Conceal me what I am, and be my aid
For such disguise as haply shall become
The form of my intent. I'll serve this Duke.
Thou shalt present me as an eunuch to him.
It may be worth thy pains, for I can sing
And speak to him in many sorts of music
That will allow me very worth his service.
What else may hap to time I will commit.
Only shape thou thy silence to my wit.   (53-62)

She consciously adopts a disguise for her maidenly protection
and to exercise the wit which women are not supposed to have.
She fits the role:

I my brother know
Yet living in my glass. Even such and so
In favour was my brother; and he went
Still in this fashion, colour, ornament,
For him I imitate.   (III.iv.370-374)

We now have all the information about the main plot that we
require, and we have received it in a very short time. What of
the subplot?

*Maria says Olivia is distressed at her uncle, Sir Toby Belch,
for his late night carousing. Sir Toby encourages Sir
Andrew Aguecheek as Olivia's suitor (I.iii).*

Olivia's grief is excessive. Sir Toby has no time for such non-sense: "What a plague means my niece to take the death of her brother thus? I am sure care's an enemy to life" (lines 1-2). Twelfth Night is the Feast of the Christmas Lord of Misrule, and backstairs at Olivia's house the subplot is moving. Sir Toby's protégé, Sir Andrew, ostensibly a suitor for Olivia but really the provider for Sir Toby's purse, is a prize simpleton. He laments his misspent education: "I would I had bestowed that time in the tongues that I have in fencing, dancing, and bear-baiting. O, had I but followed the arts!" (lines 88-91). His income is in castilians so he is probably a Spaniard — a good butt for a joke in 1600. His name is probably from Agu-chica, or "Little-wit," according to Hotson. Sir Toby's outrageous description of him — "He's as tall a man as any's in Illyria ... He plays o'the viol-de-gamboys, and speaks three or four languages word for word without book" (lines 18-25) — he has taken from Rabelais.

Toby's name was known from "Toby-night," the Biblical Toby's marital abstinence for the first night after marriage — a problem for Maria, Olivia's small gentlewoman, in love with Toby. Feste sympathizes: "if Sir Toby would leave drinking, thou wert as witty a piece of Eve's flesh as any in Illyria" (I.v.24-26). Toby hails her with, "Look where the youngest wren of nine [or mine] comes" (III.ii.63), using more folklore: the Wren is both the King of the Birds and "the tiny cave-dweller" of Saba and Mine. Toby follows with his bawdy joke about Sir Andrew's thin hair:

> TOBY: It hangs like flax on a distaff; and I hope to see
> a huswife take thee between her legs and spin it
> off.
> AND: Faith, I'll home tomorrow, Sir Toby.
> (I.iii.97-100)

Twelfth Night is also a time for dancing, the delight of Sir Andrew who *says* he is good at gambols, capers, and sprawling "kickshawses"; he even claims excellence in the acrobatic *salto indietro,* or "back-trick." And there were many games at Christmas time in Elizabethan England. Tray-trip was a form of dice where a three was the winning throw: Toby says "Shall I play my freedom at tray-trip and become thy bond slave?" (II.v.183-184); and Feste tries to beg a third gold piece of Orsino as a Christmas present with, "Primo, secundo, tertio, is

a good play ... the triplex, sir, is a good tripping measure"
(V.i.34-36) — only to be told, "You can fool no more money
out of me at this throw" (V.i.38-39). A popular implement for
dicing was the four-sided top, whirligig, by which Feste symbolizes poetic justice: "And thus the whirligig of time brings in his
revenges" (V.i.373-374). But the riddle is centre-stage in *Twelfth
Night* with Maria's cunning "dish o' poison" for Malvolio:
"M.O.A.I. doth sway my life" (II.v.106), a key to the subplot.

The Second Movement: Complications

Orsino, the lover of love, and Olivia, the lover of sorrow, sit
apart, each in splendid but ridiculous isolation, at either end
of Illyria. Viola moves between them, bringing fresh air to their
unrealities. True love, disguised and love-sick, links those hidden in romantic guises. The subplot emerges: a party begins —
to become such a confusion that we almost forget the resolu-
tion hinges on coincidence.

> *Viola is the page, Cesario, at Orsino's court. The Duke
> sends her as his love-envoy to Olivia. Aside, Viola admits
> she has fallen in love with him (I.iv).*

The effect of Viola's disguise on Orsino is like that of
Rosalind's on Orlando: men relax, if only superficially, when
conversing with other men. In three days, Orsino shows more
of his essential self to Cesario than he has to his neighbour,
Olivia, or would ever reveal to Viola as a female stranger. Nor
does Viola's sexuality seem to develop gradually; she loves her
man at once and pursues him as best she can.

Courtship envoys were customarily used by European aristocrats in the sixteenth century; for example, Henri of France
both courted and married Maria de' Medici by envoys, so
Orsino is acting with courtly decorum.

> *Olivia and her steward, Malvolio, witness Feste's fooling.
> Sir Toby delays Cesario at the gate; Malvolio cannot make
> him go. Cesario presents Orsino's suit to Olivia (she falls
> in love with him), who says he is not to call again, unless
> he comes to tell her Orsino's response. She sends Malvolio
> after Cesario with a ring which he supposedly left (I.v).*

Like Touchstone, Feste is "an allowed fool" (line 89), privileged to speak out with impunity. Bawdy wordplay is his stock response. "My lady will hang thee for thy absence," Maria tells him. "Let her hang me" he replies. "He that is well hanged in this world needs to fear no colours" (lines 3-5). Maria bids him, "Make that good [prove that statement in a decent sense]" (line 6). And Feste's answer blandly reverts to gallows humour, dismal but decent: a man well hanged by the neck "shall see none to fear." Feste logically examines the weaknesses of others, like his "proof" that Olivia is the fool. "Take the fool away," she orders. "Do you not hear, fellows?" Feste retorts. "Take away the lady,"

> FESTE: Good madonna, give me leave to prove you a fool.
>
> OLIVIA: Can you do it?
>
> FESTE: Dexteriously, good madonna.
>
> OLIVIA: Make your proof.
>
> FESTE: I must catechize you for it, madonna. Good my mouse of virtue, answer me.
>
> OLIVIA: Well, sir, for want of other idleness, I'll bide your proof.
>
> FESTE: Good madonna, why mourn'st thou?
>
> OLIVIA: Good fool, for my brother's death.
>
> FESTE: I think his soul is in hell, madonna.
>
> OLIVIA: I know his soul is in heaven, fool.
>
> FESTE: The more fool, madonna, to mourn for your brother's soul, being in heaven. Take away the fool, gentlemen.   (52-67)

When Feste says, "For what says Quinapalus? 'Better a witty fool than a foolish wit'" (lines 32-33), he talks of his absurd little figure on a stick. He is a professional, like the real Stone the Fool, whipped for calling "some lord about court, fool." Malvolio can say of Feste: "I saw him put down the other day with an ordinary fool that has no more brain than a stone" (lines 79-80), but Feste becomes Malvolio's nemesis. Olivia says,

> O, you are sick of self-love, Malvolio, and taste with a distempered appetite. To be generous, guiltless, and of free disposition, is to take those things for birdbolts that you deem cannon bullets.   (85-88)

Like others in Illyria, Malvolio has got things out of proportion.

This is our first meeting with Olivia. She was described three times as "abandoned to her sorrow" (I.iv.19), but on her first entry she allows Feste to fool her out of her mourning. Toby, drunk, delays Cesario at the gate. Sir Toby has been compared to Falstaff, but, as Feste puts it, he "has a most weak pia mater [brain]" (line 110).

OLIVIA: Cousin, cousin, how have you come so early by this lethargy?

SIR TOBY: Lechery! I defy lechery!   (118-120)

Viola, though no "comedian," is playing a temporary role as messenger. Olivia agrees to see him.

OLIVIA: Give me my veil; come, throw it o'er my face;
We'll once more hear Orsino's embassy.
[Enter Viola.]

VIOLA: The honourable lady of the house, which is she?

OLIVIA: Speak to me; I shall answer for her. Your will?

VIOLA: Most radiant, exquisite, and unmatchable beauty — I pray you tell me if this be the lady of the house, for I never saw her. I would be loath to cast away my speech; for besides that it is excellently well penned, I have taken great pains to con it. Good beauties, let me sustain no scorn. I am very comptible, even to the least sinister usage.

OLIVIA: Whence came you, sir?

VIOLA: I can say little more than I have studied, and that question's out of my part. Good gentle one, give me modest assurance if you be the lady of the house, that I may proceed in my speech.

OLIVIA: Are you a comedian?

VIOLA: No, my profound heart; and yet, by the very fangs of malice, I swear I am not that I play. Are you the lady of the house?

OLIVIA: If I do not usurp myself, I am.

> VIOLA: Most certain, if you are she, you do usurp
> yourself; for what is yours to bestow is not
> yours to reserve. But this is from my com-
> mission. I will on with my speech in your
> praise, and then show you the heart of my
> message.
>
> OLIVIA: Come to what is important in't. I forgive
> you the praise.
>
> VIOLA: Alas, I took great pains to study it, and 'tis
> poetical.
>
> OLIVIA: It is the more like to be feigned; I pray you,
> keep it in. I heard you were saucy at my
> gates, and allowed your approach rather to
> wonder at you than to hear you. If you be
> not mad, be gone; if you have reason, be
> brief. 'Tis not that time of moon with me, to
> make one in so skipping a dialogue.
>
> (I.v.170-193)

We spectators know (Olivia does not) that Viola's "I am not
that I play" gives the same status to both "the messenger" and
Cesario, whom Viola is also playing. The life of the scene
derives from the tensions of the interplay of several different
kinds of role-playing; it alerts us to the further roles involved.
Feste has called Olivia a fool for mourning her brother's death,
and Viola, when Olivia finally unveils, also disapproves:

> Lady, you are the cruellest she alive,
> If you will lead these graces to the grave,
> And leave the world no copy.   (230-232)

In the inappropriate role of mourner, Olivia is violating her
more basic role as the beautiful and eligible young woman she
reveals when she unveils. But we, in the audience, realize that
there is another parallel: Viola, too, is a beautiful and eligible
young woman. Two people share the same social role. Viola,
despite the restraints of her disguise and her duty to Orsino,
has the best perspective. She even manages to make fun of her
rival. "Is't not well done?" Olivia asks as she removes her veil.
Viola cannot resist. "Excellently done — if God did all" (line
226). When Olivia asks what Cesario would do in Orsino's
place, Viola speaks some of Shakespeare's most touching love
poetry:

Make me a willow cabin at your gate,
And call upon my soul within the house;
Write loyal cantons of contemnèd love
And sing them loud even in the dead of night;
Hallow your name to the reverberate hills
And make the babbling gossip of the air
Cry out 'Olivia!' (257-263)

Olivia is a bit sardonic; when Cesario pleads on the Duke's behalf that she marry and leave the world a copy of her graces, she says:

O, sir, I will not be so hard-hearted. I will give out
divers schedules of my beauty. It shall be inventoried,
and every particle and utensil labelled to my will. As,
item: two lips, indifferent red; item: two grey eyes, with
lids to them; item: one neck, one chin, and so forth.
(233-237)

As the meeting ends, Olivia begins to feel
        this youth's perfections,
With an invisible and subtle stealth,
To creep in at mine eyes. (285-287)

She begins to play her basic role of eligible young woman. But as another woman rather than a man inspires her performance, she is forced to play a new but inappropriate role that structurally parallels Viola's role of Cesario.

Olivia falls madly in love with Cesario. "Even so quickly may one catch the plague?" (line 284), she asks — as well she might when, in just five scenes, Orsino loves Olivia; Olivia loves Cesario (who is really Viola), and Cesario, whose true sex cannot be revealed, loves Orsino. She concludes,

Fate, show thy force; ourselves we do not owe.
What is decreed must be, and be this so. (300-301)

Viola's twin brother, Sebastian, saved by Antonio, arrives in Illyria, where Antonio has many enemies (II.i).

When Sebastian arrives the complications multiply. There are other traces of human pain here, for Antonio's relation with Sebastian has its poignancy. He is in danger near Orsino's court, but he is willing to risk that to be near his friend. Sebastian's response is virile:

My stars shine darkly over me. The malignancy of my
fate might perhaps distemper yours; therefore I shall
crave of you your leave, that I may bear my evils alone.
It were a bad recompense for your love to lay any of
them on you.

     If you will not undo what you have done ... desire it
not. Fare ye well at once ... I am bound to the Count
Orsino's court. Farewell.   (3-7, 33-38)

Sebastian is as brisk as his twin. Antonio's language, too, is
emphatic:

I have many enemies in Orsino's court,
Else would I very shortly see thee there —
But come what may, I do adore thee so
That danger shall seem sport, and I will go!   (40-43)

"Adore" is a strong word in Shakespeare. It prepares us for
Antonio's violent language when he thinks Sebastian betrays
him.

    Malvolio gives Cesario the ring. Viola realizes that Olivia
    has sent it to Cesario as a love-token (II.ii).

    The external characteristics of Malvolio are given briefly:
he holds the ring on his staff of honour with disdain; then
throws it into the street. Viola's soliloquy shows she realizes
what is happening:

I left no ring with her; what means this lady?
Fortune forbid my outside have not charmed her!

                                           (17-18)

When Viola says "Disguise, I see thou art a wickedness" (line
27), Shakespeare mocks the Puritans, whose attack on the players was based on the supposed abomination of men dressing
unnaturally as women. Viola is amused and perplexed by her
doubly ironic role:

How will this fadge? My master loves her dearly;
And I, poor monster, fond as much on him;
And she, mistaken, seems to dote on me.
What will become of this? As I am man,
My state is desperate for my master's love.
As I am woman — now, alas the day,
What thriftless sighs shall poor Olivia breathe!

O Time, thou must untangle this, not I!
It is too hard a knot for me t'untie.   (33-41)
Shakespeare shows much of Viola's character in soliloquies
and asides. Like Rosalind, Viola enjoys human freedom and
growth in male disguise; but she is more conscious of her sexual identity than are Julia and Rosalind; so the effect of the girl-
as-boy motif is different from that in *Two Gentlemen* and *As You
Like It.* Viola decides to stay in disguise. She could change back,
but at the moment she seeks freedom in the restrictions of her
disguise. Liberated from her role as a young woman, she moves
to self-discovery. Raised with a twin brother, she knows how to
adapt to her new role.

> *Sir Toby, Sir Andrew, and Feste merrily drink the night
> away. Maria warns Malvolio is coming. Sir Toby verbally
> abuses Malvolio. Maria plans a trap for him (II.iii).*

This is one of Shakespeare's great comic scenes and is well
loved by audiences. The atmosphere is given by Toby's "Not to
be abed after midnight, is to be up betimes" (lines 1-2) and "'tis
too late to go to bed now" (lines 183-184). Sir Toby wants to
"rouse the night-owl in a catch" (line 56) — a lively round in
which the melody is hurled rapidly from one singer to the next.
The catch, "Hold thy peace," is sung boisterously by Toby,
Andrew, and Feste in a drinking bout, often with hilarious stage
"business": Sir Andrew admits to being a "dog at a catch" (lines
58-59); but Maria describes the performance as "caterwauling"
(line 70). Of the Sir Tobys in living memory, Ralph Richardson
at Sadler's Wells in 1931, and Laurence Olivier at the Old Vic in
1937, are still talked about. The catch and its low comedy contrast with the plaintive music that follows Orsino. The catch is a
musical sign: it separates the subplot from the central romantic
action of the play. The musical signs identify the low characters,
heighten the impact of the romantic music of Orsino, and allow
each group to serve as a musical foil to the other.

Behind the revelry, however, is the theme of mutability.
This is the essence of Feste's famous song "O mistress mine!"
(lines 37-50). Although it is an invitation to pleasure, the song
says time destroys love and beauty:

What is love? 'Tis not hereafter;
Present mirth hath present laughter,

What's to come is still unsure.
In delay there lies no plenty —
Then come kiss me, sweet and twenty,
Youth's a stuff will not endure.   (45-50)
The singing wakes and angers Malvolio. He appears, tradi-
tionally in a nightgown, nightcap, and carrying a candle, and
his face peering round the door is an exquisite moment of the-
atrical comedy:

My masters, are you mad? Or what are you? Have you
no wit, manners, nor honesty, but to gabble like tinkers
at this time of night? Do ye make an alehouse of my
lady's house, that ye squeak out your coziers'
[cobblers'] catches without any mitigation or remorse
of voice?   (85-90)

Modern actors who have made the image of the indignant
Malvolio memorable include Donald Wolfit (many times), and
Michael Hordern at the Old Vic (1954). John Neville's reac-
tions as Sir Andrew at the Old Vic (1958) were hilarious. Sir
Toby meets Malvolio's intrusion with righteous indignation:

SIR TOBY: Art any more than a steward? Dost thou
           think, because thou art virtuous, there shall
           be no more cakes and ale?
FESTE: Yes, by Saint Anne, and ginger shall be hot
           i'the mouth, too.   (110-114)

Sir Toby labels him a Puritan, but Maria sees through
Malvolio's hypocrisy:

The devil a puritan that he is, or anything constantly,
but a time-pleaser [opportunist], an affectioned [affect-
ed] ass... the best persuaded of himself, so crammed, as
he thinks, with excellencies, that it is his grounds of
faith that all that look on him love him.   (140-145)

In this clash we have a microcosm of the puritan-cavalier issue
that was beginning to divide England during Shakespeare's
lifetime. But we must not take Malvolio too seriously in this
scene where the total effect is of fun and festival. The scene
sets up the main action of the subplot, and it deepens the character of each of the roles. "The Catch Scene" also heightens
the romantic involvement of the two main people in the comedy by contrasting its raucous jollity with the romantic beauty of
the next scene, where Viola-Cesario tells of her love for Orsino.

Orsino shares his melancholy with Cesario. Feste sings.
Orsino tells Cesario to take a jewel to Olivia (II.iv).

Orsino likes songs of love's innocence chanted by "The spinsters, and the knitters in the sun" (line 44). Feste obliges with a haunting lyric:

> Come away, come away, death,
>   And in sad cypress let me be laid.
> Fie away, fie away, breath!
>   I am slain by a fair cruel maid.   (50-53)

This pokes fun at the death-from-unrequited-love cliché. Feste then says to Orsino, "Now the melancholy god protect thee, and the tailor make thy doublet of changeable taffeta, for thy mind is a very opal" (lines 72-74).

Orsino shares his experience to teach his young companion. Cesario's responses reveal that other lessons are learned. Orsino confesses that

> boy, however we do praise ourselves,
> Our fancies are more giddy and unfirm,
> More longing, wavering, sooner lost and worn,
> Than women's are.   (32-35)

Orsino's melancholy and self-centredness are part of his lack of awareness and half the joke. He unconsciously contradicts himself:

> There is no woman's sides
> Can bide the beating of so strong a passion
> As love doth give my heart; no woman's heart
> So big to hold so much, they lack retention.
> Alas, their love may be called appetite,
> No motion of the liver, but the palate,
> That suffers surfeit, cloyment, and revolt.
> But mine is all as hungry as the sea,
> And can digest as much. Make no compare
> Between that love a woman can bear me
> And that I owe Olivia.   (92-102)

Viola quietly responds, "Ay, but I know." She unconsciously knows that many differences between men and women are dissolvable. But she says she knows

> Too well what love women to men may owe.
> In faith, they are as true of heart as we.
> My father had a daughter loved a man —

> As it might be perhaps, were I a woman,
> I should your lordship.   (104-108)

The charming little fiction leads to one of the great passages in the play: Viola's poignant description, in the third person, of her own enforced silence. In response to Orsino's "And what's her history?" she says:

> A blank, my lord. She never told her love,
> But let concealment, like a worm i'the bud,
> Feed on her damask cheek. She pined in thought,
> And with a green and yellow melancholy,
> She sat like Patience on a monument,
> Smiling at grief. Was not this love indeed?
> We men may say more, swear more, but indeed
> Our shows are more than will; for still we prove
> Much in our vows, but little in our love.   (108-117)

As the twin of a male, she knows that, apart from physical attributes, men and women are both similar and different.

> *Maria puts a forged letter in Malvolio's way, which he imagines is written by Olivia (supposedly in love with him); he is watched by Sir Toby, Sir Andrew, and Fabian. Malvolio is prompted to do all that the letter suggests (II.v).*

The subplot's second great comic set-piece is known in the theatre as "The Garden Scene" (or "The Box-Tree Scene"), as behind this tree the plotters watch Malvolio read the false letter. The tree, in fact, is the only scenery absolutely necessary to the play.

In his stupendous conceit Malvolio imagines himself Count Malvolio, the husband of Olivia. As Maria says, "he has been yonder i'the sun practising behaviour to his own shadow this half-hour" (16-17). "Having been three months married to her," Malvolio imagines,

> sitting in my state ... Calling my officers about me, in
> my branched velvet gown, having come from a day-bed,
> where I have left Olivia sleeping.... And then to have
> the humour of state; and after a demure travel of
> regard — telling them I know my place, as I would they
> should do theirs — to ask for my kinsman Toby....
> Seven of my people, with an obedient start, make out

for him. I frown the while, and perchance wind up my watch, or play with my *[touches his steward's chain an instant, and then starts]* — some rich jewel.   (43-60) The stage direction, surely right, was suggested by Brinsley Nicholson. Maria puts in his path a cryptic letter which is in Olivia's forged handwriting. "'I may command where I adore ... M. O. A. I. doth sway my life'" (lines 103-106). "If I could make that resemble something in me" (lines 117-118), he thinks. Maria has cleverly chosen the signs of the elements whose initials appear in his name: Mare-Sea, Orbis-Earth, Aer-Air, and Ignis-Fire. M. O. A. I. This riddle is an essential part of the joke on Malvolio. The use of "a-dore" is also a joke. A riddle and plot to make someone look foolish was a Court pastime for which the current slang was to *dor* someone, or to give someone the *dor* (borrowed from the Dutch: *een door,* a fool). Shakespeare introduces it previously with one of the Sir Andrew's echoes:

SIR TOBY: She's a beagle true bred, and one that
adores me — what o'that?
SIR AND: I was adored once too.   (II.iii.172-174)

Malvolio decides that Olivia is the author and he the intended recipient since all the initials are in "Malvolio." He reads on ...

'In my stars I am above thee, but be not afraid of greatness. Some are born great, some achieve greatness, and some have greatness thrust upon 'em. Thy fates open their hands, let thy blood and spirit embrace them ...'
(II.v.139-143)

Maria has skilfully used Malvolio's own thoughts, ambitions, and literary style. The illusion is that Olivia's feelings are like his own. "'Let thy tongue tang arguments of state. Put thyself into the trick of singularity'" (145-147) — he is instantly convinced.

The letter scene in the garden is a sheer delight, and Malvolio's behavior is so exquisitely preposterous that we laugh at him as he goes to carry out the letter's instructions: to come to her smiling, and in yellow stockings and cross-garters.

After some fooling with Feste, Cesario meets Olivia who declares her love for him (III.i).

Viola, conscious she is a woman in man's clothes, is often witty in half-concealed sexual quips. When Feste hopes Jove will reward Cesario with a beard, she says, "By my troth, I'll tell thee, I am almost sick for one *[aside]* — though I would not have it grow on my chin" (lines 45-47). To Feste foolery "does walk about the orb like the sun, it shines everywhere" (lines 37-38).

We have known of Olivia's feelings for Cesario, but we are pleased when she succumbs to Cesario despite his refusals. This is partly because we know that Sebastian is waiting in the wings to provide her with a way out of her dilemma.

Fabian and Sir Toby convince Sir Andrew to write a challenge to Cesario (III.ii).

Antonio gives his purse to Sebastian in case he wishes to buy something (III.iii).

Malvolio enters in yellow stockings and cross-garters, and he is smiling. Olivia tells Maria to have him looked after by Sir Toby, who, with Fabian, decides to shut him in a dark room like a lunatic. Sir Andrew arrives with his challenge and waits for Cesario in the orchard. Olivia gives Cesario a jewel and her picture. Sir Toby delivers Sir Andrew's challenge to Cesario, and the duellists draw. Antonio, mistaking Viola for her brother, offers to take Cesario's place. Sir Toby draws, but the officers arrive, recognize Antonio and arrest him. He asks Cesario for his purse back; she denies she had it but now wonders if her brother is alive. Sir Toby and Fabian egg on Sir Andrew to follow Cesario and fight him (III.iv).

Olivia values Malvolio. She says, when she thinks he is really mad, "I would not have him miscarry for the half of my dowry" (63-64).

Manoeuvered into a fight with Sir Andrew, Cesario is terrified. "Pray God defend me!" she exclaims in a double-entendre to the audience. "A little thing would make me tell them how much I lack of a man" (293-294). The foolish knight is also a rank coward. "For Andrew," Sir Toby observes, "if he were opened and you find so much blood in his liver as will clog the foot of a flea, I'll eat the rest of the anatomy" (III.ii.58-60). It is thus good fun when Sir Toby manipulates him into fighting his supposed rival. The danger here is that the director might descend to farce instead of the rich comedy, when two cowards try to duel. Sir Andrew is *very* grateful to his fellow coward for the chance to put the swords away.

Antonio's speech about Viola to the Officers is impassioned:

ANT: Let me speak a little. This youth that you see
      here
      I snatched one half out of the jaws of death;
      Relieved him with such sanctity of love;
      And to his image, which methought did
      promise
      Most venerable worth, did I devotion.

1 OFF: What's that to us? The time goes by. Away!

ANT: But O, how vile an idol proves this god!
      Thou hast, Sebastian, done good feature
      shame.
      In nature, there's no blemish but the mind;
      None can be called deformed, but the unkind.
      Virtue is beauty; but the beauteous evil
      Are empty trunks o'er-flourished by the devil.

1 OFF: The man grows mad; away with him.

(350-362)

Everyone mistakes Sebastian for Cesario. Sir Andrew strikes him and gets more than he expected. Sir Toby draws. Olivia stops the fight, asking Sebastian indoors (IV.i).

Although the revels are over, Shakespeare does not therefore neglect two other features of the ancient Christmas festival. In this scene he gives us a mixture of the folk-play and the sword-dance, or the mock-combat, in the scuffle between Andrew, Toby, and Sebastian.

Malvolio, locked in a dark room, is visited by Maria, Sir Toby, and Feste who fetches him writing materials and a light (IV.ii).

Also part of the Twelfth Night festival was the mumming. In Shakespeare's version Feste dresses up as the counterfeit Sir Topas, the curate. As he dons a gown to impersonate the curate, he comments, "and I would I were the first that ever dissembled in such a gown" (lines 5-6). He visits "Malvolio the lunatic" (lines 21-22). Today, we feel that this is no jest: madness is no longer comic to us. But it was to the Elizabethans, who flocked to Bedlam for amusement. Great care is required of the stage director, therefore, or the sympathies of the modern audience will veer towards the victim, which is not Shakespeare's intention. The scene should be played lightly, with a rich sense of *joie de vivre*, so that the audience can appreciate the excellent fooling of Feste, rankling from Malvolio's earlier insults, with his two voices: alternately as himself and as the curate Sir Topas come to exorcise the "hyperbolical fiend" (line 25) that vexes the lunatic. He finds more "evidence" that Malvolio is deranged:

FESTE: Sayst thou that house is dark?

MALV: As hell, Sir Topas.

FESTE: Why, it hath bay windows transparent as barricadoes, and the clerestories toward the south-north are as lustrous as ebony. And yet complainest thou of obstruction!

MALV: I am not mad, Sir Topas. I say to you, this house is dark.

FESTE: Madman, thou errest. I say there is no darkness but ignorance, in which thou art more puzzled than the Egyptians in their fog.

MALV: I say this house is as dark as ignorance, though ignorance were as dark as hell. And I say there was never man thus abused. I am no more mad than you are — make the trial of it in any constant question.

FESTE: What is the opinion of Pythagoras concerning wildfowl?

MALV: That the soul of our grandam might haply inhabit a bird.

FESTE: What thinkest thou of his opinion?

MALV: I think nobly of the soul, and no way approve his opinion.

FESTE: Fare thee well; remain thou still in darkness. Thou shalt hold the opinion of Pythagoras ere I will allow of thy wits, and fear to kill a

woodcock lest thou dispossess the soul of
thy grandam. Fare thee well.   (33-59)
Maria, who started it all, sees that the Clown's stage costume
has no function: "Thou mightst have done this without thy
beard and gown; he sees thee not" (lines 63-64). Sir Toby, who
has been a prime mover in the gulling of Malvolio, confesses
he is uneasy about what has been done:

> I would we were well rid of this knavery. If he may be
> conveniently delivered, I would he were, for I am now
> so far in offence with my niece that I cannot pursue
> with any safety this sport the upshot.   (66-70)

*Olivia asks Sebastian to marry her, and they go with a
priest (IV.iii).*
Olivia bids Sebastian,

> Now go with me and with this holy man
> Into the chantry by; there before him
> And underneath that consecrated roof
> Plight me the full assurance of your faith ...   (23-26)

Sebastian, reaping the reward of passion stirred up by Cesario,
accepts:

> For though my soul disputes well with my sense
> That this may be some error, but no madness,
> Yet doth this accident and flood of fortune
> So far exceed all instance, all discourse,
> That I am ready to distrust mine eyes,
> And wrangle with my reason that persuades me
> To any other trust but that I am mad —
> Or else the lady's mad....   (9-16)

As he is a pragmatic young man without the romantic delusions that suffuse Illyria, he rushes off to marry Olivia.

The appearance of the priest is one of a number of references to religion and the Church in the play. Earlier, when
Olivia first admits Cesario, she catechizes him:

> OLIVIA: We will hear this divinity. Now, sir, what is
>   your text?
> VIOLA: Most sweet lady —
> OLIVIA: A comfortable doctrine, and much may be
>   said of it. Where lies your text?
> VIOLA: In Orsino's bosom.

OLIVIA: In his bosom! In what chapter of his bosom?
VIOLA: To answer by the method, in the first of his
          heart.
OLIVIA: O, I have read it; it is heresy.   (I.v.211-218)

Feste is more practical:

VIOLA: ... Dost thou live by thy tabor?
FESTE: No, sir, I live by the church.
VIOLA: Art thou a Churchman?
FESTE: No such matter, sir; I do live by the church.
          For I do live at my house, and my house
          doth stand by the church.   (III.i.1-7)

Shakespeare also hints at the Gospels in the handling of the "possessed" Malvolio as though he were the demoniac Gadarene [Mark 5.6] . Sir Toby vows, "If ... Legion himself possessed him, yet I'll speak to him" (III.iv.84-86); Feste rebukes the "dishonest Satan" (IV.ii.31), and when asked to read out the message from that unclean spirit, he does it according to Gospel.

The Third Movement: Resolution

All occurs in the generalized "place" [see *End Notes*] — the exterior of Olivia's house — and in one long scene (V.i). Although Shakespeare's remarkable economy ties up all the loose ends cleanly, there are moments when he nods: Antonio stands around the stage with nothing to do for a long time — an unusual lapse; the motivation for Orsino's change of heart from Olivia to Viola is not quite satisfactory; and the treatment of Malvolio, adequate in Shakespeare's time, without care can be a little strong today.

> *Feste jests with Orsino. Antonio arrives, guarded; he denies he is a pirate and accuses Viola of being a thief after being friends for three months. Viola has been at court for this time, so Orsino thinks he is lying (V.i.1-129).*

After Feste has begged for his Christmas present of gold from the Duke, Antonio tells of how his "love" has been met with in gratitude:

A witchcraft drew me hither.
That most ingrateful boy there by your side
From the rude sea's enraged and foamy mouth
Did I redeem; a wrack past hope he was.
His life I gave him, and did thereto add
My love without retention or restraint,
All his in dedication. For his sake
Did I expose myself — pure for his love —
Into the danger of this adverse town;
Drew to defend him when he was beset;
Where, being apprehended, his false cunning —
Not meaning to partake with me in danger —
Taught him to face me out of his acquaintance,
And grew a twenty years' removèd thing
While one would wink ...   (74-88)

*Sebastian has not returned; Olivia accuses Cesario of
breach of promise (V.i.129-170).*

When Olivia makes her accusation, Orsino reproaches
Cesario, thinking that the boy he has befriended has treated
him as he (supposedly) treated Antonio. The parallelism is
comic and prevents us from taking Antonio's plight too seriously. Orsino banishes Cesario using another old Twelfth Night
custom: Hunt the Fox. The ritual of "killing the old Devil for
good luck" involved hunting and killing a fox or a cat released
in the court. This ritual gives point to Feste's earlier defiance
of Malvolio: "Sir Toby will be sworn that I am no fox, but he
will not pass his word for twopence that you are no fool"
(I.v.74-76). Orsino banishes that young fox, Cesario, in similar
terms:

O thou dissembling cub! What wilt thou be
When time has sowed a grizzle on thy case?
                                        (V.i.162-163)

With Antonio before us, we are reminded that affection puts a
man in another's power.

*Sir Andrew and Sir Toby are beaten by Cesario (actually
Sebastian). All realize the two are twins. Olivia marries
Sebastian; Orsino and Viola will marry (V.i.170-270).*

The bloody coxcombs given to Toby and Andrew by Sebastian have sobered both the drunkards. One result, the Clown later tells us, is that Maria's success with the false letter has got Sir Toby to the altar; "In recompense whereof, he hath married her" (line 362).

When Sebastian appears, Shakespeare reminds us of androgyny in disguise. On stage, Viola is metaphorically Viola *and* Sebastian simultaneously (the ancient man-woman of the Mummers' Plays), and she is free to act out her full self. Shakespeare, by giving Viola this metaphor in her dialogue with Olivia — "my speech," "my part," "I am not that I play" — develops the idea that Viola is Viola-Sebastian but without a penis (III.iv.293-294; see above). This metaphor shows the power of playing: as Viola-Cesario she charms Orsino; as Sebastian-Cesario she charms Olivia. And the audience is delighted to share with Viola her recognition of her emotional self — "I am almost sick for [a beard]" (III.i.45), "I am no fighter" (III.iv.237), and "I am one that had rather go with Sir Priest than Sir Knight" (III.iv.264-265). In playing and disguise, social barriers are broken, and she and we get to know the essential Viola-Sebastian.

When Sebastian arrives, the apparent problems of sexual delusion are solved, and a happy ending becomes natural. Over the three months of the play, Orsino develops his liking of Cesario without having to cope with Viola's sex. Olivia's decision to marry Sebastian is only seemingly sudden. She, too, has had three months to know Viola-Sebastian; only when Sebastian enters does sex (i.e. marriage) enter her stated plans. Because Viola and Sebastian are twins, Olivia has not really been deceived. Sebastian says:

> So comes it, lady, you have been mistook.
> But nature to her bias drew in that.
> You would have been contracted to a maid.
> Nor are you therein, by my life, deceived:
> You are betrothed both to a maid and man.
>
> (V.i.256-260)

Olivia and Orsino began the play imprisoned by gender, but have changed. Stimulated by Viola's disguise, they have grown up. The situation is resolved by the formula of romantic comedy: Olivia marries Sebastian, a clone of the Cesario who stole her heart; Orsino, having lost Olivia, transfers his devotion to Viola, a woman once more.

The stage problem of twins (which occurs in *The Comedy of Errors* as well as *Twelfth Night*) is usually solved by players who resemble each other; they do not have to be physically identical. Having exactly the same costume is usually sufficient, together with the two players rehearsing "mirror games" and similar improvisational exercises so that their stage movement is similar.

The Duke's seemingly inexplicable shift from Olivia to Viola shows what many believe to be the play's central idea: *the instability and contradictory nature of love;* the havoc it creates has implications far beyond the immediate situation of Illyria. Orsino does ultimately change. Although he has yet to discover himself in the process, he does discover that Viola-Cesario is really a woman and he admits her into his world:

> Give me thy hand,
> And let me see thee in thy woman's weeds.
>
> (lines 269-270)

This is all he has to say. Since he has only known Viola as his page, the change to loving her as his "mistress" is abrupt.

> *Feste brings a letter from Malvolio, and he is sent for.*
> *Olivia identifies the writing of the trick letter as being*
> *Maria's and promises Malvolio justice; he says he will be*
> *revenged. Exeunt; Feste sings (V.i.275-405).*

Malvolio writes and speaks in his own defence in dignified language; he is not a bit artificial. "Madam, you have done me wrong; Notorious wrong" (lines 326-327) is his cry to Olivia when he is brought from the darkness of his cell to the bright end of the comedy. Feste reminds him:

> Why, 'Some are born great, some achieve greatness,
> and some have greatness thrown upon them.' I was
> one, sir, in this interlude, one Sir Topas, sir — but that's
> all one. 'By the Lord, fool, I am not mad!' But do you
> remember: 'Madam, why laugh you at such a barren
> rascal, an you smile not, he's gagged?' And thus the
> whirligig of time brings in his revenges.   (368-374)

Malvolio's final words, "I'll be revenged on the whole pack of you!" (line 375), leave us uneasy. Once the whole plot against him has been exposed, Olivia pities him and condemns the jest: "Alas, poor fool! How have they baffled thee!" (367). After Malvolio's exit she declares, "He hath been most notoriously abused" (line 376).

The ending is a startling shift of viewpoint. The Duke calls Viola "Orsino's mistress and his fancy's queen," and we are securely in the *play world*. Then suddenly it is the epilogue: we are with Feste among toss-pots and their drunken heads. This abrupt transition is bridged by music, but Feste's song is bitter; it is not a traditional ending. He sings that the Fool's "tiny wit" lies in the contrast between two "foolish things": his profession- al bauble and a phallus. The song runs through a rake's progress of lechery, drunkenness, and rejection by society, which has been the case since "A great while ago the world begun." He ends by reminding us that he is an entertainer — a player as well as an imaginary character:

> our play is done,
> And we'll strive to please you every day.   (404-405)

But this epilogue to *Twelfth Night* has an epilogue of its own in *King Lear.* There we find an additional stanza for the song:

> He that has and a little tiny wit,
> With heigh-ho, the wind and the rain,
> Must make content with his fortunes fit,
> Though the rain it raineth every day.   (*Lear* III.ii.74-77)

BOYS AS WOMEN

With women's parts played by boys, Shakespeare drew on the paradox of a boy player acting the role of a young woman wear- ing the disguise of a boy. This could produce complicated sexu- al overtones, and the effect was increased by the Elizabethan anger against homosexual feeling. With boys playing women's roles, overt homosexual reference was hazardous in the the- atre. We are more than usually conscious in *Twelfth Night* of the sex of the players, the sex of the roles they are playing, and the double disguise of the boy playing Viola. It is all in jest, but it cannot be too light-hearted because Shakespeare suggests that Viola is not. She says:

> Disguise, I see thou art a wickedness
> Wherein the pregnant enemy does much.   (II.ii.27-28)

When a boy playing a girl becomes emotionally involved with a boy playing a girl disguised as a boy, sexual distinctions begin to dissolve. This Elizabethan convention was very particular: it was not a convention like (say) the "principal boy" of the English pantomime. Viola was played, and was meant to be played, by a boy. Shakespeare's audience saw Cesario without effort as Orsino sees him; more importantly they saw him as Olivia sees him; indeed it was (the boy playing) Olivia they had most to believe. This affects the sympathy and balance of the love scenes of the play: the delicacy of the dialogue between Orsino and Cesario is dramatically right; and the more outspoken passion of the scenes with Olivia is right. In the theatre, I discovered (Leeds, 1952-54) that when boys play the parts of women the notion of love is taken into a rarefied atmosphere beyond sexual appetite. Modern audience members accept the convention, provided it is accepted by the players, and believe Olivia is in love with a young man. This is right for *Twelfth Night.*

In modern productions the use of actresses for the women's parts alters the problem. Sexual relations become more "natural." If Olivia and Cesario are played by women, we can be less moved by the love relationship, and the power of the poetry decreases. Actors must take great care because the audience tends to believe that Viola-Cesario is a girl, and then Olivia may appear dim-witted.

THE PROBLEM OF MALVOLIO

The so-called problem of Malvolio is not Shakespeare's problem at all. It was created by Charles Lamb in the *Essays of Elia.* He said, "I confess that I never saw the catastrophe of this character, while Bensley played it, without a kind of tragic interest.

"This statement was highly influential: we have seen that Irving made the play Malvolio's tragedy, and that modern productions can interpret Malvolio as a tragic figure. Lamb's view has bedevilled the issue until the present day.

Twelfth Night is *not* a tragedy, and Malvolio, despite his suffering, is not a symbol of human greatness. In the theatre Malvolio *is* humiliated. Today, an audience cannot see pompous people stripped of their status without sharing their embarrassment: it is too easy to laugh at Malvolio, and so, we feel we have done harm, and we feel guilty. This is the effect on a modern audience of practical jokes. But for Shakespeare, Fortune is represented by the clever and engaging Fool, before whom stands a humiliated petty tyrant who talks of revenge. Malvolio does not profit from his lesson but, as he angrily leaves, stiffens his self-love by his sense of injured merit.

Yet there is more to it than that. Malvolio is the gull in the comic subplot: a distorting mirror of the main plot. Orsino, Olivia, and Malvolio mistake dreams for life; they all, in their own way, practise before their own shadows. When Olivia tells Malvolio that he is "sick of self-love," she also speaks of herself and Orsino. To the Elizabethans they are three melancholics. The melancholy of Malvolio is his fantastic ambition. He is not in love with Olivia. Rather, he dreams of marrying her in order to become the lord of her house: he constantly sees himself in that exalted position. Such a change in rank would have seemed to the Elizabethans ridiculous to a level we can hardly appreciate.

The actor playing Malvolio must balance the emphasis between two-dimensional medieval Pride and three-dimensional character. There is no evidence that Shakespeare felt any tenderness for him, as he obviously did for Launce, Bardolph, Mistress Quickly, Master Slender, Don Armado, Dogberry, and some of his other fantastics. He draws Malvolio's character distantly, with little or no sympathy. Shakespeare's intentions are clear. Malvolio has the defects of his qualities: lack of humour, intolerance of the pleasures of life, a belief in the priority of order and respectability, and a strong conviction that he, Malvolio, is born to put everything right. When he cries, "Jove, I thank thee!" after reading the forged letter, he shows a preposterous intimacy with the Almighty. Such a person, in Shakespeare's comic world, cannot be tragic but is merely the object of other people's fun.

FESTE, THE FOOL

Feste is a different kind of Fool from Touchstone, although they were probably both first created by Robert Armin. The two Fools perform essentially the same function, but there are major differences. Despite Touchstone's commitment to Audrey, he remains somewhat detached from his surroundings. Feste can be actively involved in the dramatic events or, as in the epilogue, become fully alienated. Touchstone's *forte* is highly sophisticated parody. Feste's is plain speaking. Touchstone is a slow clown who, although he would deny it, comes into his own in the Forest of Arden; Jaques in particular appreciates him. Feste is a quick clown, yet often quite alienated from Illyria. Clear-eyed and wise, he is separated from the absurd human world about him; even while he is part of it, he comments on such follies. He knows that foolery walks "about the orb like the sun": he exposes the illusions of Orsino and Olivia and, above all, those of Malvolio who is his specific target. As Sir Topas, Feste interviews the "lunatic" Malvolio, and makes us realize the fine line between the mad and the sane. To remain sane, Feste wears a clown's mask against the infection of Illyria. It is no accident that he sings of the wind and the rain, like Lear's Fool. They are remarkably alike when, in *play worlds* where everyone is slightly mad, motley is a badge of knowledge. Like all Fools, Feste is obscene. Traditionally, the Fool has an excess of virility, symbolized by his bauble: "A fool's bauble is a lady's playfellow," was a common phrase.

Feste is Shakespeare's most musical Fool: "the fool has an excellent breast" (II.iii.18). A member of Olivia's household, he is borrowed by Orsino to supply his music. He is full of songs and wit: "A sentence is but a cheveril glove to a good wit; how quickly the wrong side may be turned outward!" (III.i.11-13); and "No indeed, sir, the Lady Olivia has no folly. She will keep no fool, sir, till she be married, and fools are as like husbands as pilchers are to herrings; the husband's the bigger. I am indeed not her fool, but her corrupter of words" (III.i.31-35).

THE LOVERS

Viola is Shakespeare's most warm and human heroine. A joy to perform, she is the focus of the play. She and her twin brother, each a clone of the other, are the non-Illyrians who bring a sense of reality into a world where everyone is self-deluded. To operate effectively there, Viola must use a disguise: a form of acting which, necessary for her to survive, frees her. Her playing, in fact, symbolizes the play. William Hazlitt rightly said that Viola is the great and secret charm of *Twelfth Night*. We have a friendship for Sir Toby; we patronize Sir Andrew; we have an understanding with the Clown, a sneaking kindness for Maria and her rogueries; we feel a regard for Malvolio, and both sympathize with and laugh at his gravity, his smiles, his cross garters, his yellow stockings, and his imprisonment. But what gives us a stronger feeling than all this is Viola's confession of her love.

It is right that Viola should marry Orsino, but we are not sure if it is right for him to marry her, particularly when in his last words he calls her "Orsino's mistress and his fancy's queen." Orsino is

> Of great estate, of fresh and stainless youth,
> In voices well divulged, free, learned, and valiant,
> And in dimension and the shape of nature
> A gracious person.   (I.v.248-251)

But he is also narcissistic: he is so blinded by self-love that he is not aware that he is obsessed by fancy, not reality. What he loves is his romantic idea of the lover of which he is the exemplar. He worships at a distance and woos by proxy. Even his anger is idealized:

> Why should I not — had I the heart to do it —
> Like to th'Egyptian thief at point of death
> Kill what I love — a savage jealousy
> That sometime savours nobly?   (V.i.115-118)

But he does learn, if only a little. Orsino alters from being an entirely self-centered man to a prospective bridegroom, and he changes from Olivia's lover to Viola's.

The Countess Olivia's wallowing in "a brother's dead love" is as delicately unreal as Orsino in his love of her. The Fool cracks her idealism, and one visit from Cesario shatters it. Olivia turns from recluse to ardent lover. Her new obsession is even more absurd (although she does not know it) because it rests upon a more fundamental error. When her Cesario turns out to be Sebastian, she does not stop loving him, because the twins are identical.

THE GROTESQUES

Twelfth Night is full of great roles for actors. Theatrically, Sir Andrew and Sir Toby are a comic unity. Sir Andrew's imposing list of follies, both natural and acquired, makes him the world's fool. The "thin-faced" Sir Andrew is a theatrical relation of Slender in *The Merry Wives*, and they were probably played by the same actor; but he has little of Slender's attractiveness. Sir Toby delights in Sir Andrew's stupidity and in his "three thousand ducats a year" (I.iii.20) which he helps him spend; indeed, Fabian calls him Sir Toby's "manikin" (III.ii.51) because the knight manipulates him like a puppet.

Although Sir Toby has a searching eye for other people's foibles, he is usually too drunk to recognize his own. He hates "A false conclusion!... as an unfilled can" (II.iii.6). He is a gentleman by birth who was a soldier, and has some half-forgotten learning: he speaks Spanish at one time (I.iii.39), French at another, and Latin at a third (II.iii.2); he speaks of contemporary physiology; he talks theology when drunk; and he discusses "philosophy" (i.e. science). As Sir Toby emerges in performance, I agree with Harley Granville-Barker when he says that he is not a bestial sot.* He is a poor relation, and it is the boredom of Olivia's house, where she sits solitary in her mourning, that drives him to his jolly companions. At the end, however, Sir Toby remains what he was before, a drinker and parasite. Yet with Maria as his wife there is some hope for him.

Maria, the "wren," was written for a particular actor of no great height but with sharp intelligence. She serves Olivia as her gentle-woman, but it is entirely her plot, an exceedingly clever one, that traps Malvolio; she is both the dramatist and the stage director of this playlet. Her patience has not always been noted: but she has been waiting for some time for Sir Toby to sober up, and, when he does, he realizes his good fortune and marries her at once.

Two roles are not precisely drawn but very rewarding for performers to "fill out": Fabian and Antonio. Fabian is likely "the yard man," or the head stable-lad, of Olivia's house,

---

* Granville-Barker (1912): 4.

because his talk is about horses and dogs. Among the practical jokers, he is the cautious one; but he has the courage to speak up before Olivia at the end. He treats Sir Andrew with a certain respect, but as he does not treat Sir Toby as his senior, Granville-Barker does not think he is a young man. Antonio is drawn from the Elizabethan seaman-adventurers, like Drake. A "notable pirate," and "salt-water thief," Orsino calls him.

> A baubling vessel was he captain of,
> For shallow draught and bulk, unprizable;
> With which, such scatheful grapple did he make
> With the most noble bottom of our fleet,
> That very envy and the tongue of loss
> Cried fame and honour on him.   (V.i.51-56)

Much of the role appears to be context-based, drawing its colour from the particular time and place, which means little to modern audiences.

COMIC CHANGE IN ILLYRIA

Despite the delusions of the Duke, the Countess, and Malvolio, Illyria has a great charm. It is just Malvolio who is not good natured; and only his gulling gives us a feeling of unease, which it would not have done in Shakespeare's time. Illyria is the perfect setting for such a romantic comedy: two lovely houses, a seashore, and the shade of the tree are quite sufficient to create a memorable world. It exists nowhere except in some relaxed, sun-soaked days we all remember from our past. We have all lived in Illyria, and we recognize ourselves and others we know in these delightful and amusing people whose delusions we might share, might we not?

They speak prose that is mostly simple and straightforward. They are likely to produce both fine-sounding words and puns (Shakespeare could resist neither) which delight us as they flow by in the theatre. The verse is regular, lyrical in its style, with a quality that lingers in the mind. While Granville-Barker was right in saying that it should be spoken swiftly, as in all Shakespeare's plays, in *Twelfth Night* specifically it requires considerable variation both between and within scenes. We have noted the difference in pace in the first three scenes of the First Movement, and there are many other possible examples.

As to variations within scenes, an example is the first duet of Olivia and Cesario. It should proceed briskly; however, the audience requires some signals that the Countess is falling in love with the messenger. Thus the enthusiasm of Viola's "If I did love you in my master's flame" (I.v.253ff.) should be tempered by a slightly slower pace in her "Make me a willow cabin at your gate" (I.v.257ff.), which provides Olivia with time to register her feelings. These variations exist throughout the play and require the closest attention by the director and the players, because, in many instances, they signal change.

Toward the end of *Twelfth Night*, as in *As You Like It*, the people fulfil their potential: they assume their proper roles and true identities. Both Viola and Sebastian do so in full; they act out their growth so that, with them, we have a sense of completion. Orsino and Olivia do not change in such a way: they commence as deluded, and they only find themselves because of the pressure of dramatic events — centered on Viola's disguise, the active agent of change in Illyria. Nevertheless, at the finale the Duke and the Countess are somewhat different from what they are at the beginning of the play, and both have the potential for further growth with the spouses they have chosen. Malvolio, Sir Andrew, and Feste do not change: Malvolio learns nothing. Sir Andrew is too deeply immersed in his private world ever to change. Sir Andrew cannot learn anything, and Feste probably knew it all already. Feste cannot come out from behind his mask to dramatize his identity; he conceals this role-fixity not only from the others but even (almost) from himself, because, simultaneously, he must conceal it from us, the audience. And when we hear that Sir Toby has married Maria we know that they, too, are well on their way to realizing their potential.

But the most significant change upon which Shakespeare's comedies focus is not individual. Critics like Northrop Frye focus on the discovery of personal identity in the comedies * or, like Anne (Righter) Barton, concentrate on self-discoveries or a deepening and development of personality.** This is

---

* Frye (1949).
** Righter (1982).

important at the level of the individual player. But for the director, the audience, and the reader, the important changes in the comedies are collective rather than individual. Both occur: the transformations that the individual members of the society undergo reveal a process that takes place within the social unit as a whole.

In the theatre, Shakespearean comedy alters the *play world;* it is never the same at the end as it was in the beginning. To Shakespeare, dramatic action has specific power: it opens up a society that was previously closed in on itself. By the end, all the significant characters have more freedom than they did; and this happens because dramatic action has altered their context. In *Twelfth Night,* Viola's wearing of disguise is the dramatic action that begins the transformation of Illyria. Some people discover things about themselves at the level of the plot, or they do not (e.g., Malvolio). Those who do may change at the level of individual psychology (e.g., Viola, Orsino, Olivia), or they may not (e.g., Sir Toby, Maria). Sir Toby, if he does change, does not do so profoundly, although he is for the first time under control. It is three of the four lovers — Olivia, Orsino, and Viola (perhaps even Sebastian) — who engage in self-discovery. The degree of change among the different people indicates the various transformations of the society of the *play world.*

In *Twelfth Night,* the social transformation is primarily that of love. We begin with Orsino and Malvolio as the victims of self-love, and Olivia is deluded in her mourning-love for her brother; Sir Andrew's impossible love is not love at all, Maria's love is unrequited, and Sir Toby loves his cups more than he loves her. Sebastian has not thought about it, and Feste looks at it all dispassionately. At the end, only Malvolio, Sir Andrew, and Feste have not altered their relationship to love.

CONCLUSION

Twelfth Night is Shakespeare's most entertaining comedy. Besides the music and the merriment which one of the greatest of all Fools provides, the play has a splendid variety of comic elements that entrance audiences. Illyria is Shakespeare's most distinctive place; it has a unique atmosphere that envelops the audience. As well as the delicately ironical scenes, full of lovely poetry, such as Viola's duets with Orsino and Olivia, Illyria includes some of Shakespeare's most brilliantly drawn people. There are the less subtle but no less entertaining scenes: the singing of the catch and Malvolio's arrival in the middle of the night, the forged letter with the revellers hiding in the tree, Malvolio's appearance before Olivia in yellow stockings and cross-garters, the mock duel between Sir Andrew Aguecheek and Viola-Cesario, and Malvolio in the dark house — five of Shakespeare's most uproarious and richly comic scenes, and all quite different from one another. All are broader than the love scenes, yet they are not farce. The whole is a true comedy: the audience is entertained, laughs a lot, and goes home feeling good about itself. And what people recall is their delight in the theatre and, perhaps unconsciously, the dangers of personal delusion.

The director should also remember that the play was created as an entertainment for Christmas time. There are hosts of references to seasonal folklore, games and rituals. Yet, paradoxically, the atmosphere is not chilly and cold, like an English winter. *Twelfth Night* conveys a sunny and radiant feeling, as if Shakespeare's Christmas celebrations were meant to recall the happy days of summer.

THE MERRY WIVES OF WINDSOR

SIR JOHN IN LOVE

*T*he *Merry Wives of Windsor* is one of the world's great "theatre pieces." Most literary critics are not fond of it, because there is little poetry, and what there is cannot be regarded as Shakespeare's best. Theatre historians are intrigued by its many textual problems. But actors and directors relish it, and audiences can split their sides with laughter.

The Merry Wives is Shakespeare's most uproarious comedy. It was supposedly written as a result of the Queen's request for a play showing Sir John Falstaff in love. As Dr. Johnson said, "Falstaff could not love, but by ceasing to be Falstaff." Unlike any other Shakespeare comedy, it is a farcical romp about the aspiring middle class. Karl Marx found "in the first act alone more life and movement than in all German literature." This interesting view is difficult to maintain.

Most literary critics have thought the Falstaff in this play but a pale shadow of the great comic figure in *Henry IV*. Theatre critics have not agreed, and actors desperately want to perform Sir John. There are three significant factors in this issue. First, *this is a play for an occasion: Halloween.* Thus it is full of misunderstandings, deceptions, and counter-deceptions. Falstaff lusts after Mistress Ford as well as after her money, and she and her friend Mistress Page make a fool of him three times: he hides in a dirty clothes-basket and is dumped in the River Thames; he has to dress as a woman (like the Man-Woman of the folk plays); and at a village frolic in Windsor Castle he is disguised as Herne the Hunter with antlers — like the shaman or the horn dancers at Abbots Bromley — and he is mocked, pinched, and scorched by "fairies" like an ancient scapegoat. But Dr. Johnson was right: Falstaff cannot love except by ceasing to be Falstaff. He counterfeits love not for the pleasure but for the money. He pretends to be in love because he is hard up:

> I will be cheaters to them both, and they shall be exche-
> quers to me. They shall be my East and West Indies,
> and I will trade to them both.   (I.iii.64-67)

Falstaff is not "infatuated" at all, but is the victim of the disease that he also suffers from in *2 Henry IV:* an incurable "consumption of the purse."

Second, *this is a farcical comedy.* Farce, *sui generis,* is a mixture of dialogue and physical action — with a higher proportion of action than in other dramatic genres. Critics who wish to analyze *The Merry Wives* as just "literature" twist the play into something it is not. Readers must extend their imagination greatly if they are to catch the spirit of a farcical comedy. Take a famous example:

> FAL: Pistol!
> PIS: He hears with ears.   (I.i.137-138)

Little is conveyed to the reader from the words on the page of the physicality involved here. Falstaff and his companions from London are used to Pistol — probably the most outrageous figure in all comedy, with his gross over-statements and gestures like an "old time" actor — so they do not react to what he says. But this is not so with the Welshman, Evans. How does he react when he sees Pistol's huge theatrical gesture, and hears the loud, rolling voice declaim: "He hears with ears"? Disbelief — astonishment — and perhaps a short silence before, in his Welsh lilt, Evans says: "The tevil and his tam! What phrase is this, 'He hears with ear'? Why, it is affectations" (I.i.139-140). Perhaps Evans might react with "a double take" before he speaks? This will depend on the actor. There is nothing of this in the text, and the reader must create it all by imagination. This is only a very simple example. Just think of the possibilities when Falstaff hides in a dirty clothes-basket! Or when Evans acts as a fairy, and Pistol is a hobgoblin!

Third, *Falstaff is as he should be when he is out of his element* — among the bourgeois of Windsor instead of at the Boar's Head in Eastcheap. If there is a difference in Falstaff, it lies not in him but in the plays themselves, for here he is in a country town and is not involved with the great people of the realm and their serious business. He is in a different context from that of *1 & 2 Henry IV.*

The Merry Wives is a roistering middle-class comedy, with strong farcical elements. It is Shakespeare's nearest approach to the rural humour of the English folk tradition.

TEXT AND SOURCES OF THE PLAY

This play, so much the delight of theatregoers, is a bane to scholars. Its text, sources, and date of composition are all matters of great controversy. The director, using the text of the First Folio, can ignore some, but not all, of the problems. But when read instead of staged, *The Merry Wives* raises question after question. Why do a set of characters from the history plays *(Henry IV* and *Henry V)* appear in the script? Why does Shakespeare take such care to paint a historically accurate portrait of Windsor in the 1590s in this, his sole play dealing entirely with contemporary English life? Why even select Windsor as the locale for a play about country life, when Shakespeare knew Warwickshire so well? Why, when he had already produced masterful poetry in other plays, does he write a play almost entirely in prose, with a little verse that is inferior? What source did he use for the play?

The Merry Wives of Windsor was first published in 1602 in a corrupt version ("Q1"), later reprinted with a few alterations in 1619 ("Q2"). Q1 is about twelve hundred lines shorter than the Folio text: it omits and transposes scenes, cuts the parts of William and Robin and all references to the Court and Order of the Garter, and mangles many individual passages. The best text is that of the First Folio ("F1") of 1623. But given the historical information we have, it is likely that the play in F1 is an amalgam of texts performed at different times.

There is no known direct source for the play, but there are countless examples of similar plots in classical, medieval, and Renaissance sources; Shakespeare could have remembered his plots from his reading over a period of years. Renaissance Italian novellas include several duped lovers who, like Falstaff, have three trysts with the wife of a jealous husband, and the young maiden sought after by three suitors (the Anne Page story) is constant in conventional Italian comedy. Thus, there is scholarly consensus that, if there was a precise source, it was a work based on Italian models.

The stage tradition about the hurried composition of *The Merry Wives* has led some scholars to think Shakespeare must have reworked an old play in his company's repertory. This play is called, for convenience, the *Ur-Merry Wives*.

Three good candidates have been identified for sources: a tale published in 1558 in Ser Giovanni Fiorentino's *Il Pecorone* (Day I, Novella 2); "The Tale of the Two Lovers of Pisa" from Tarlton's *Newes out of Purgatorie* (1590); and *Of Two Brethren and Their Wives* (1581) by Barnaby Riche. In the latter, a married woman has three suitors. Two, the doctor and lawyer, are comic types whom she dupes. But the plots could also have come from many *commedia dell'arte* or *commedia erudita*-type plays. All the story details found in *The Merry Wives* plots were known in both narrative and dramatic form by 1590 — several years before the creation of *The Merry Wives* — and were commonly known to audiences of the time.

Shakespeare may have inserted various topical events. The Sir Thomas Lucy story is a familiar one: as a youth, Shakespeare was prosecuted for stealing deer from a park that belonged to Sir Thomas Lucy of Charlecote, near Stratford; Shakespeare wrote a scurrilous ballad about Lucy and fled to London; and in *The Merry Wives* Falstaff is a deer-stealer, while Justice Shallow represents Lucy. Scholars have argued for years over the horse stealing and the presence of Germans in the play but without success. Much of the confusion may be because Shakespeare makes fun of living people.

HISTORY OF THE PLAY

The occasion of the first performance is also controversial. The popular tradition is that Queen Elizabeth I saw *1 Henry IV* at Court (late 1596 or early 1597) and, having so enjoyed Sir John Falstaff, she wanted to see the fat knight in love. So Shakespeare wrote a third Falstaff play, *The Merry Wives*, at great speed. There is no documentary evidence for this tradition before 1702, and we shall likely never know the truth — but it is a delightful story just the same.

The first performance of *2 Henry IV* possibly took place in late 1598. *The Merry Wives* might have followed in April, 1599. Evidence suggests that *The Merry Wives* and *2 Henry IV* may have been composed at the same time. Despite the Queen's command, in *The Merry Wives* Falstaff is not in love: he counterfeits love for both wives to gain money — so that "they shall be exchequers to me" (I.iii.65).

From its connections with the *Henry IV-Henry V* plays, it is usually assumed that *The Merry Wives* was performed around 1598-1600. The first performance may have been at Windsor Castle, at what has become known as a "grand affair." Different evidence supports the alternative view that the play was first performed at Whitehall on April 23, 1597 (St. George's Day), at the Feast of the Order of the Garter: Lord Hunsdon, just appointed Lord Chamberlain (and thus patron of Shakespeare's theatre company), received the Order.

The first *record* of a performance is in the Revels Accounts for 1604. There is no reason to doubt the title-page of the Q1 that the play had been acted "divers times," both for the Queen "and elsewhere." All these traditions could be true, even if the text used in some performances was not yet that of F1.

After the Restoration in 1660, *The Merry Wives* was one of the first plays to be acted, but Pepys did not like it. A special performance "at Court at St. James'," on 23 April, 1704 or 1705, had a great cast including Betterton, Gogget, Mrs. Barry, and Anne Bracegirdle. An attempt to "improve" the play for early eighteenth-century audiences by Dennis, *The Comical Gallant: Or the Amours of Sir John Falstaffe,* was presented at Drury Lane in 1702 but was not successful. In the 1720s, other versions became popular and continued so for two centuries, though often in an abridged form. Quin excelled as Falstaff, though Kemble (at first) and Kean preferred to play Ford. Kean's Mistress Ford was Ellen Tree. Ellen Terry and Mrs. Kendal later played the wives, with Beerbohm Tree as Falstaff. The play was also performed in America, in Philadelphia, as early as 1770, and by 1773 in New York, and it was never quite lost thereafter.

There have been many successful revivals in the twentieth century. Experimental productions included Oscar Asche's surprisingly unpopular 1911 "wintry" version, and his calamitous

1929 modern dress variation (Anne rode pillion on Fenton's motor-bicycle); Komisarjevsky's in 1935 was set in Vienna; and in a Yale Shakespeare Festival 1953 it was acted in the language of Shakespeare's day, coached by Helge Kokeritz. Famous modern Falstaffs include Paul Rogers (Old Vic, 1955), Anthony Quayle (Stratford-upon-Avon, 1955), Joss Ackland (Old Vic, 1959), William Hutt (Stratford, Ontario, 1978), and John Woodvine (Stratford-upon-Avon, 1979). Orson Welles played Falstaff in his movie, *Chimes at Midnight* (1966), in which he combined parts of all three Falstaff plays.*

FORM

Shakespeare may have added some personal satire of living people within the roles of Shallow and even Slender. He put in the compulsory romance with "sweet Anne Page" and her wooer Fenton, who, by carrying her off in spite of less worthy suitors favoured by otherwise likeable parents, fulfils the clichés that, if "the course of true love never did run smooth," "love will prevail." Falstaff's three undoings are all broad and farcical. Yet *The Merry Wives* is not primarily satiric comedy, intrigue comedy, or romantic comedy. Nor is it strictly a farce, but it is farcical.

The Merry Wives has a form unique in Shakespeare's plays: it is a "citizen's comedy," with large farcical elements. This genre was made famous by others: Dekker in *The Shoemaker's Holiday;* Chapman, Jonson, and Marston in their *Eastward Ho* (and Webster and Dekker in the rival comedies *Westward Ho* and *Northward Ho*); and later by Middleton and by Massinger. Primarily this form is about urban middle-class life. Whereas many Shakespearean comedies have women disguised as men, this is his only play where a man is disguised as a woman. The two effects are radically different on stage. The boy acting Viola dresses as Cesario: the character maintains the charm of Viola but becomes pathetically vulnerable. A man dressed as Falstaff who is dressed as the old woman of Brainford, however, is ridiculous — which epitomizes the differences between Shakespeare's warm and rich comedies and *The Merry Wives*.

---

* For theatre history see Oliver (1971), Sprague (1944, 1953), Sprague and Trewin (1970), and Whittaker (1956).

Shakespeare presents a delightful and charming portrait of life in an Elizabethan English country town in this play. We come to know the town of Windsor and its own small world. Hawking and greyhound racing are important. We can smell the hot venison pasty and pippins and cheese. It is a "raw rheumatic day," and there are fires in the grates. We go into the Garter Inn. Nearby are the Thames, Datchet Mead, Windsor Castle and its chapel; and, at midnight, we meet under Herne's Oak in Windsor Little Park. Yet this is all incidental. As always, Shakespeare is most interested in people. We can peek into the private lives of the townsfolk — as diverse a group of people as we could find anywhere. Money and marriage are their concern, not kings and crowns. Shakespeare is at his very best when he unifies the locale and the people, as when Mistress Quickly tells us what it is like to be Caius's housekeeper: "I keep his house; and I wash, wring, brew, bake, scour, dress meat and drink, make the beds, and do all myself" (I.iv.93-95). At night, she enjoys "a posset" with the manservant, Rugby, "at the latter end of a sea-cole fire" (I.iv.7-9). And at Hallowmass, Slender lent his Book of Riddles to a certain Alice Shortcake. Shakespeare's Windsor is a fully realized *play world*.

THEME, PLOT AND STRUCTURE

Compared with other Shakespearean plays, *The Merry Wives* is relatively unsophisticated, as befits a citizen's comedy. Its major theme, appropriate for a comedy with this form, is *Nature vs. civilization*. This appears in a variety of ways:

plain "honesty," or virtue	vs.	sophistication
townsfolk	vs.	the gallant or courtier
"true love"	vs.	a marriage of convenience

But it is also complex and incongruous in terms of Falstaff who is seen as:

the "real" Falstaff
    Falstaff as he sees himself
        Falstaff seen by Mistress Page and Mistress Ford
        all Falstaff's disguises

Shakespeare was a master at structuring multiple activities in his plays, making his audiences aware that there are worlds within worlds. In *The Merry Wives* there are three plots. *The surplot* links the play to the "grand affair" at Windsor Castle. In F1, which may or may not be the text of the first performance, Shakespeare included material for the occasion, and for his patron's own election to the Order of the Garter. He changed the locale from an Italianate original to Windsor, a plausible setting for middle-class characters, and one with immediate Garter links for an Elizabethan audience. Many items in the surplot are left hanging, as if they were additional to an original text. Shakespeare also added a compliment to the Queen, knowing that she would be at the special performance.

The main plot is the Falstaff-in-love story, in which he is unsuccessful in his designs on Mistress Ford. This story also provides the major structure: the three short plays of the linen-basket, the female impersonation, and Herne the Hunter. In the main plot we meet a pair of prosperous townsmen — Ford given to extreme jealousy, and Page — whose lively wives prove quite capable of dealing with a fat, old, lecherous counterfeit from London. There is a rich collection of characters: a happy, hearty country innkeeper whose evenness of temper can be upset only by a major calamity, like the theft of his post-horses; Mr. Justice Shallow, who, curiously, has moved from Gloucestershire to Windsor; Mistress Quickly, who, even more curiously, has a new and different role as a good-hearted housekeeper, skilled as a go-between; Bardolph, Nym, and Robin, Falstaff's page, who are the visiting group from London; and a Welsh parson, Sir Hugh Evans, who is better at giving a Latin lesson than fighting a duel. Evans may have been based on a Thomas Jenkins who was the master of Stratford-on-Avon's Grammar School from 1575 to 1579, a period when the young Shakespeare may have been there.

The subplot is a romance comedy. The traditional sweet young maiden — Mistress Anne Page, the picture of "pretty virginity" — is in love with her handsome true love Fenton. There is an elaborate deception whereby she marries him against the wishes of her parents: her mother favours the Frenchman, Dr. Caius, a choleric French physician who draws his patients from among the gentry and royalty; and her father has promised her to the well-to-do Slender, the shy nephew of Shallow. Together with the Welsh parson Hugh Evans, Dr. Caius mangles the English language, and Anne certainly does not want to marry him:

> Alas, I had rather be set quick [alive] i'th'earth,
> And bowled to death with turnips.   (III.iv.84-85)

Shakespeare blends the three plot lines smoothly, integrates his characters organically with events, and places them in a fast-paced context. Dr. Caius moves from plot to plot: three times in I.iv. he tells us he is on his way to the "grand affair," the Windsor Castle ceremony. Mistress Quickly acts as go-between in both the main and subplots; she is strongly instrumental in unifying them. The intrigues — the tricks played on Falstaff, and the outwitting of Page and his wife, Caius, and Slender, by Fenton and Anne — are skilfully linked when Fenton's success is revealed to prevent the Pages from gloating further about their exposing of Falstaff. The audience leaves joyous: laughing over the fractured English of Evans and Caius, amused by the antics of Bardolph and Nym, chuckling at the malapropisms of Mistress Quickly, happy with the escapades, and content that the heroine has got her hero and that middle-class morality has been successful. Above all, they have laughed *with* Falstaff, and laughed *at* him.

It is not surprising, with so many "comics" — and particularly if the play was in fact written hurriedly — that the plotting should not be as tight as usual. Nothing comes of the charge of killing deer brought by Shallow against Falstaff at the beginning of the play, and no more is heard of the ridiculous threat to make a Star Chamber matter of it — it seems to have been a "false start" to the play.

The structure of the play has been carefully composed for presentation on the most simple stage. Most of the action occurs in the "place" [see *End Notes*]. A hiding place of some kind is required for various purposes: the hiding of Simple from Caius (I.iv); the "arras" behind which Falstaff stands (III.iii); and the "chamber" into which Falstaff steps (IV.ii). The upper stage is not used. Thus *The Merry Wives* could easily have moved from public stage, private theatre and Court, with a minimum of trouble.

Shakespeare's prime aim in *The Merry Wives* is to entertain. He tries to make everyone happy: Queen Elizabeth, by fulfilling her wish to see Falstaff in love; Lord Hunsdon, his patron, by prefiguring Hunsdon's own installation at Windsor; and the theatrical public, by bringing before them one of the freshest sets of characters in Elizabethan comedy as well as, on stage, upholding the virtue of English women. As Mistress Page says,

> We'll leave a proof, by that which we will do,
> Wives may be merry, and yet honest too.   (IV.ii.98-99)

ACTION

In the main plot, Sir John, who fancies himself a ladies' man (actually it is money he is after), sends duplicate love letters to Mistress Ford and Mistress Page. The result is a picaresque structure: three linear Movements, each a separate playlet linked with the others.

The First Movement: The Linen-Basket Play

The merry wives are to teach Falstaff a lesson. Assisted by Quickly, they arrange a tryst between Falstaff and Mrs. Ford at the latter's house. Ford (disguised as "Brook") hears Falstaff boast of his impending tryst and burns with jealousy. When Ford bursts in, hoping to catch his wife in the act, Falstaff is stuffed in a basket of dirty linen and dumped into a ditch by the river Thames (I.i-III.iii).

At the very opening, we hear that Falstaff has been up to his same tricks again: " ... If he were twenty Sir John Falstaffs, he shall not abuse Robert Shallow, Esquire" (I.i.2-4). And when he arrives, he is his old self:

> SHALLOW: Knight, you have beaten my men, killed
> my deer, and broke open my lodge.
> FALSTAFF: But not kissed your keeper's daughter?
> (I.i.105-107)

He complains to Pistol, much as he complained to Bardolph in *1 Henry IV,* of the style of life he must resort to:

> I, I, I myself sometimes, leaving the fear of God on the
> left hand and hiding mine honour in my necessity, am
> fain to shuffle, to hedge, and to lurch ...   (II.ii.22-24)

Falstaff, short of funds, hopes to get his hands on Ford's money by pretending love for the one who holds the purse-strings, his wife. Ford, as Brook, learns of his plans and resolves to "detect" his wife and "be revenged" on the fat knight. Falstaff, Ford and his wife are each out to outwit the other two but are unaware of the other's intentions. So, when Falstaff says his first words to Mistress Ford, "Have I caught thee, my heavenly jewel?" (III.iii.40), they are brilliantly comic.

Shakespeare shows conclusively, in the words of Mistress Page, that "wives may be merry, and yet honest too." The two women are far from the submissive wives recommended by the social theories of the age and by Katherine in The Shrew. They are independent, enterprising women who even control their husband's purse-strings. They are indeed "honest," in the sense of "chaste," and in their loyalty to, and understanding of, each other. But they cannot be solemn even about that: when Ford says to Mistress Page, "I think, if your husbands were dead, you two would marry," he receives the reply he deserves: "Be sure of that — two other husbands" (III.ii.13-15). There is no ambiguity in their attitude to Falstaff's letters; it is summed up in one phrase, "What doth he think of us?" (II.i.78). Their only other thought is, "Let's be revenged on him" (II.i.87).

Mistress Ford declares that she will "consent to act any villainy against him" (II.i.91-92) that still allows her to be honest. As often in Shakespeare, the word "act" quickly possesses a theatrical meaning, and, when Mistress Ford and Mistress Page plan the first of their deceptions, they invoke the idea of the play.

MRS. F: Mistress Page, remember you your cue.
MRS. P: I warrant thee. If I do not act it, hiss me.
(III.iii.35-36)

So, with her husband at the door, Mistress Ford bundles Falstaff into the linen-basket which servants carry out as Ford searches the house. It is this scene which, for Falstaff, ends so unpleasantly in the cold waters of the Thames. Mistress Page says it is to cure him of his "dissolute disease" (III.iii.179).

But no sooner has this episode ended than the merry wives plan to play more tricks upon Falstaff and to send for him at eight o'clock the next morning.

The Second Movement: The Female Impersonation Play

At a second assignation, again interrupted by Ford,
Falstaff disguises himself as the fat woman of Brainford,
receives a vigorous beating from Ford, and finally escapes
(III.iv-IV.iii).
Meanwhile the subplot is proceeding. The incredibly shy
Slender, who exemplifies "intellect flickering with its last feeble
glimmer,"* makes his "proposal" to Anne:

SLEN: Now, good Mistress Anne —
ANNE: What is your will?
SLEN: My will? 'Od's heartlings [God's little heart],
          that's a pretty jest indeed! I ne'er made my
          will yet, I thank heaven. I am not such a sickly
          creature, I give heaven praise.
ANNE: I mean, Master Slender, what would you with
          me?
SLEN: Truly, for mine own part, I would little or
          nothing with you. Your father and my uncle
          hath made motions. If it be my luck, so; if not,
          happy man be his dole. They can tell you how
          things go better than I can.   (III.iv.54-63)

"Good mother," Anne pleads, "do not marry me to yond fool"
(III.iv.81). We sympathize with her.

    Reflecting upon his sojourn in the river, Sir John laughs at
himself. At his size, whatever the water, "If the bottom were as
deep as hell, I should down" (III.v.11-12). Ironically enough,
Falstaff employs a rather airy play image of his own. He and
Mistress Ford had (at least in his account) embraced, kissed,
and, "as it were, spoke the prologue of our comedy" (III.v.69)
when the raging husband made his appearance. Thus, like
Mistress Ford, Falstaff regards the encounter in terms of a
play. Unfortunately for him, however, while he thinks himself
the dramatist of the meeting, it is controlled by the merry
wives.

    Of Falstaff's retelling to Ford of his ducking in the Thames
(III.v. 75-113), it is no exaggeration to say that there is no finer
comic prose in the whole of English drama. He is outraged as

---

* Boas (1968) 298.

he describes to the disguised Ford the sensation of being crammed in the laundry-basket:

> and then, to be stopped in, like a strong distillation,
> with stinking clothes that fretted in their own grease.
> Think of that, a man of my kidney — think of that —
> that am as subject to heat as butter; a man of continual
> dissolution and thaw.   (III.v.102-106)

In the second of the three playlets in which Falstaff's greed and lust involve him, he is forced to adopt a disguise by "counterfeiting the action of an old woman" (IV.v.109). He escapes and providently saves himself from Ford. In his soliloquy, Falstaff says,

> I would all the world might be cozened, for I have been
> cozened and beaten too. If it should come to the ear of
> the court how I have been transformed, and how my
> transformation hath been washed and cudgelled, they
> would melt me out of my fat drop by drop, and liquor
> fishermen's boots with me. I warrant they would whip
> me with their fine wits till I were as crestfallen as a dried
> pear.   (IV.v.85-92)

Later, explaining to "Brook" how, as the fat woman of Brainford, he was thrashed by Ford, Falstaff reveals his old talent for equivocating:

> I will tell you: he beat me grievously, in the shape of a
> woman; for in the shape of man, Master Brook, I fear
> not Goliath with a weaver's beam, because I know also
> life is a shuttle.   (V.i.18-21)

Ford, of course, knows that Falstaff's story is part-fiction being told to him as "Brook," who is totally fictional.

The horse-stealing in the fourth act is not part of either plot, and it disappears from the play as mysteriously as it came. The key character is a German Duke who never appears but whose men make off with three of the Host's post-horses. An offshoot of the surplot, it is so weak that it disintegrates. Circumstantial evidence shows that the German Duke was Frederick, Duke of Wurtemberg, elected to the Order of the Garter in 1597, who since 1592 had been obsessed with a desire for the Order, badgering Elizabeth and her courtiers. Finally the Queen in 1597 agreed. Then the Duke began his campaign for investiture and installation, necessary for full Garter membership. This was so serious by the summer of 1597 that Emperor Rudolph II barred the English Merchant Adventurers from the German empire. The Queen died in 1603, and, when James I came to the throne, the Duke was invested in Stuttgart on November 6, 1603. The following April his proxy was installed at Windsor. Duke Frederick's activities were known in court circles and over twelve years would have been known by many Londoners.

In the horse-stealing incident, the "duke de Jamany" (IV.v.80) may be Frederick *plus* the post-horse idea taken from a scandal in September, 1596. Le Sieur Aymar de Chastes, Governor of Dieppe, returning to France from an embassage to England, was en route to the coast. Through misunderstandings, he abused the authority of his warrant and, with his retinue, tried by force to take post-horses from an innkeeper in Gravesend. He also got into difficulty with hackneymen from Rochester for attempting to take post-horses beyond the stage for which they had been hired. Since Shakespeare could not lampoon so distinguished a man as de Chastes, he turned him into another foreigner who could safely be satirized: the Duke of Wurtemberg. Having written the material, Shakespeare probably could not integrate it into the other plots in the available time, so he left it.

The Third Movement: "The Herne the Hunter Play"

> *Ford and Page are let in on the fun, and all join together to humiliate Falstaff. A third rendezvous is arranged for Windsor Park, where Falstaff, disguised as Herne the Hunter and wearing a buck's head, is pinched and burned by an assortment of characters disguised as satyrs, hobgoblins, and fairies (IV.iv-V.v).*

The third play, the comedy of Herne the Hunter, unfolds in the wintry darkness of Windsor Park. This plot also necessitates costume, not only for Falstaff but for all the other actors as well. It is a carefully prepared and executed fantasy in which
                    Fat Falstaff
Hath a great scene.   (IV.vi.16-17)
He himself is unaware of his role, or even of the fact that a play is afoot, somewhat like Christopher Sly in *The Shrew*.

As to the mumming, a good deal of careful planning goes into the performance; we are given details of the costumes, the rehearsals, and the properties, together with a brief but enchanting picture of Parson Evans, disguised as a satyr, marshalling a troupe of small children and calling, "Trib, trib, fairies. Come. And remember your parts" (V.iv.1-2).

The playlet is considerably more complicated, as well as more formal, than the two which have preceded it. Like the play scenes in *Love's Labour's Lost* and *The Dream*, the Herne the Hunter interlude represents another of Shakespeare's experiments with a play within a play relating illusion and reality [see *End Notes*]. In Windsor Park, however, it is the illusion which triumphs. Like Bottom and his friends, or the Worthies of *Love's Labour's Lost*, the actors who participate in the interlude are amateurs, and many of them are also comic figures. Yet their performance is completely successful. Falstaff is deceived as planned, and so are we, the audience in the theatre. Despite all the preparations that have gone before, and our knowledge of how this scene must end, it is hard to watch it and not forget — unless the actors deliberately "mug" their lines — that the Fairy Queen is only Mistress Quickly, and the Hobgoblin is really Pistol. (Pistol? As the Hobgoblin? The mind boggles at the theatrical possibilities.)

The Queen sets the tone in her invocation to

You moonshine revellers, and shades of night,
You orphan heirs of fixèd destiny....   (V.v.38-39)

There are times when the world cannot easily be distinguished from the stage. In Windsor Park, the previously semi-realistic play is turned into a kind of courtly masque. There people can step out of their main roles to play other parts, particularly for the purpose of compliment, in proper masque style. The park on a winter's night with its huge leafless oaks, the dark meadows and the silhouette of the castle hovering over it, is strange enough to be magical. Falstaff's confusion of the play with reality becomes all too understandable, and the spectators are actually encouraged, "in despite of the teeth of all rhyme and reason" (V.v.125-126), to share his delusion.

Then, suddenly, Falstaff recognizes "that Welsh fairy" (V.v.81) — an uproarious moment — which brings the scene swiftly back to earth. At last Falstaff gets the point. "I do begin to perceive that I am made an ass" (V.v.119). Having threatened the domestic stability of Windsor, he has become its scapegoat. Having tried to cuckold Ford, he has been exposed to general derision with the horns of a cuckold on his own head. He turns to Evans and says:

> Have I lived to stand at the taunt of one that makes fritters of English? This is enough to be the decay of lust and late-walking through the realm. (V.v.141-144)

Falstaff's face is saved, after the Herne the Hunter sequence, when the disclosure is made that those who have played tricks on him have themselves been deceived. The *play world*, if it is allowed to masquerade as reality, cannot be treated with impunity. It has its own power, and can behave in unforeseen ways and, even, deceive its creators. Like *Hamlet* to which it is close in date, *The Merry Wives* is filled with affirmations of the power of illusion. It reminds the theatre audience that life is constantly discovering within itself bewildering similarities to drama.

Falstaff is gulled as expected, but so, to their own amazement, are four of the dramatists of the Herne the Hunter comedy: Page and his wife, Caius, and Slender. Page's invitation to Falstaff to laugh at Mistress Page falls flat. Indeed, nobody can really laugh at anybody else. It is Master Fenton, after all, who steals away Anne Page.

But now the masque has faded away, the people of the main play step forward again, and all are seen for who they truly are — except they are actors on a stage. So who *is* real? The conclusion of *The Merry Wives* is one of Shakespeare's finest achievements, a great dramatist's wonderful feat of sleight-of-hand.

FALSTAFF

A great deal of nonsense has been talked about the Falstaff of this play by armchair critics. It has been said, for example, that he is a pale shadow of his previous self, that he has become a mere butt for a farce. Yet for those of us who have acted Sir John, he is the same person in all the plays in which he appears. For the audiences in the theatre, witnessing his escapades, there is no such gap as has often been alleged between the original Falstaff and the person who can easily be made to look foolish by the kind of honest woman of whom he has little experience. The man who ran away at Gadshill *[1 Henry IV]* is frightened of being found by a jealous husband. In *The Merry Wives* he pretends to be in love in order to get money, and in *1 Henry IV* he goes to war for the same reason. His letter to Hal in *2 Henry IV* (II.ii.136ff.) is written by the same man who, in *The Merry Wives*, writes:

> ... I love thee. I will not say, pity me — 'tis not a soldier-
> like phrase — but I say, love me. By me,
>> Thine own true knight,
>> By day or night,
>> Or any kind of light,
>> With all his might
>> For thee to fight,
>>> *John Falstaff.*   (II.i.10-18)

In addition to the hilarious scene when he tells Ford of his Thames adventure, Falstaff has several other comic speeches. To the actor, this "gross fat man" with "a pudding in his belly" has the same energy, the same love of life, and the same unmitigated gall wherever he appears. Falstaff plays many roles through the three plays, but here he performs a different role from any he has played before — the romantic lover — in the hope of "earning" money. To perform in this role he needs new skills, different from those he uses in other roles. But he makes as bad a lover in *The Merry Wives* as he makes a hero at Shrewsbury.

The fun in *The Merry Wives* lies in the ways in which he is victimized. The laughter of the audience comes partly from the conflicts of character with the farce-like action, and partly from the lies that "this same fat rogue" tells of his adventures — he lies about his success with Mistress Ford as he lies about the men in buckram suits after Gadshill. In *The Merry Wives*, however, he tells the truth more often than was his wont.

But the greatest laughs come from the unique idiom in which he tells both lies and truth. We know for certain that the Falstaff of *The Merry Wives* is the same person who appears in *1 & 2 Henry IV* from how he talks. We hear it on his entrance in answer to Shallow's accusations: "I will answer it straight. I have done all this. That is now answered" (I.i.109-110). Shallow, of course, is flabbergasted. As the play begins, then, the fat knight is our old acquaintance in his lusty, domineering, and blustering manner, which he uses to outface Shallow and Slender. He continues in the same way. The Falstaff of the Boar's Head who complains of his circumstances is the same Falstaff who says:

> ... you may know by my size that I have a kind of alacrity in sinking. ... the water swells a man, and what a thing should I have been when I had been swelled! I should have been a mountain of mummy.   (III.v.10-16)

With Falstaff, we laugh because of who he is.

It is true that he faces some changes. After all, Windsor is neither Eastcheap nor the Battle of Shrewsbury, and Ford and Page are neither Hal nor the Lord Chief Justice. But once the action proper gets under way (I.iii) we discover that he has some unsuspected qualities. This may result from Shakespeare's reworking of the role of a scholar or pedant from the *Ur-Merry Wives*. Thus the Host says to him, "Speak scholarly and wisely" (I.iii.2-3); Ford, in his disguise as Brook, notes, "Sir, I hear you are a scholar" (II.ii.174) and goes on to say, "you are a gentleman of excellent breeding, admirable discourse, of great admittance, authentic in your place and person, generally allowed for your many warlike, courtlike, and learned preparations" (II.ii.217-221). Cleverly, Shakespeare uses his source to make Ford sarcastic. When Falstaff uses such lurid phraseology as, "Mistress Ford ... I see you are obsequious in your love, and I profess requital to a hair's breadth" (IV.ii.1-3), he is imitating the Renaissance lover. This "fat-kidneyed rascal" is noted for his ability to counterfeit in many situations, so we are not surprised that he can do so in this context. But primarily the reprobate remains his old expostulatory self. Realizing that Welshmen were mocked for their use of the English language and their love of toasted cheese, Shakespeare has Falstaff say, "Am I ridden with a Welsh goat, too?... 'Tis time I were choked with a piece of toasted cheese" (V.v.136-138).

There is one difference between the Windsor Falstaff and the one from Eastcheap: in *The Merry Wives*, unlike *1 Henry IV*, the merry rogue is unsuccessful in turning the tables when he has been discovered. That inability brings him much nearer to the Falstaff of *2 Henry IV* who finds he cannot be resurrected once Hal finally rejects him.

But the company that marches with Falstaff into Windsor is not the same as it was in Eastcheap. Mistress Quickly is a totally different person from the Hostess of the Boar's Head and is now a warm and garrulous go-between. And Bardolph, Nym, and Pistol are treated badly by Shakespeare; he simply uses them for their eccentricities before writing them out of the script.

THE WIVES

The wives are lively and sprightly, with sharp wits. Unlike women in similar Italian comedies, they exercise their considerable powers of invention not to deceive their husbands but to support their marriage vows and deliver a lesson to the old villain who threatens communal morality. By cleverly inverting an ancient plot, Shakespeare gives it new life and places the highest value on the marriage tie. Mistress Ford and Mistress Page may make bawdy jokes, but they are steadfast in their bourgeois morality. Falstaff, "this greasy Knight," has no chance against them.

Shakespeare makes Mistress Ford and Mistress Page types of revengers, lampooning the revenge play. The wives are not satisfied with one revenge against Falstaff, they must have three. The last, a type of masque, was the traditional end to a revenge play. The wives bring it all off with great élan — far better, in fact, than most of the serious revengers.

The wives are a delight to act. Shakespeare's theatrical tour de force in the creation of the wives is that he provides only the briefest of characteristics to differentiate between them. He leaves their personalities open, relying on the boy performers, who would have altered when the play toured. As a result, they are two of the greatest comic roles for modern female performers, who can grow with them in rehearsals. They are like a breath of fresh air in the middle of the comic chaos. In the twentieth century there have been many fine performances of the two wives.

HUMOURS

In *The Merry Wives* there is some influence of the comedy of humours. But how far did this influence go? Shakespeare uses the term "humour" in his early comedies, including *Love's Labour's Lost* (III.i.23-24), and, in *The Shrew*, it frequently appears. He may have been indebted to Thomas Nashe, in whose work the word appears many times, and who may have coined "humorously" and "humorist," or to John Lyly, who, in his plays, had used the word to name phases of character. George Chapman, in *The Blind Beggar of Alexandria*, one of the most popular plays of 1596, used "humour" to indicate extreme conduct or mood; indeed, the Spaniard Bragadino is comic partly because he over-uses the term. He provides a precedent for Nym's torturing of the word in *The Merry Wives*. Chapman and Ben Jonson went beyond the mere word and extended it to the dramatic method of basing characters on "humours." This method Jonson made his own in *Every Man in his Humour* (1598), in which Shakespeare acted, and *Every Man Out of his Humour* (1599). Jonson created a formula for this method: the comic person had only one mannerism or eccentricity; this mannerism, related to others, generated dramatic action.

In this sense, *The Merry Wives* is clearly *not* a humours comedy. It is true that Nym abuses the word, and Pistol, because his speech is created from popular theatre, might possibly be thought of as a "humours" character. But Nym and Pistol have many other qualities, and neither can be reduced to one dimension. If *The Merry Wives* was later than Jonson's *Every Man in his Humour* (which is likely), then the portraits of the jealous husband Thorello and the country fool Stephano might have been Jonson's attempts to demonstrate to Shakespeare how such humours ought to be given in Ford and Slender. All that *The Merry Wives* and Chapman's (probably contemporaneous) *An Humorous Day's Mirth* have in common is that both misuse the word "humour," and both involve a jealous husband.

Shakespeare adapted the "humours" method to his own ends. Unlike his other comedies of this period, *The Merry Wives* emphasizes one predominant characteristic of each character.

Yet this technique is not exclusively that of the "humours" tra-dition. As any actor knows, the more farcical the play, the fewer dimensions the characters have. *The Merry Wives* includes more farcical elements than is usual for Shakespeare, and this broad style affects the characters of the people.

In *The Merry Wives,* a key element of a humours comedy is missing: the savage bite of Ben Jonson. He was a moralist trying to strip away the mask of hypocrisy from humanity. This Shakespeare does not do; not even Falstaff is stripped bare. The follies and vices of the others are not held up to scorn and ridicule. As the performers expose the weaknesses of Ford or Caius or Slender, they do so with gentleness and compassion. *We understand why they are as they are,* as we do with virtually all Shakespeare's people. Even Nym and Pistol do not receive their just desserts. That Shakespeare is able to graft small ele-ments of humours comedy onto the plots of *The Merry Wives* is another tribute to his skill and artistry.

HUMOURS AND ROLES

The actor of Pistol discovers that he is basically the same person he is in *2 Henry IV,* a blusterer full of sound and fury who cre-ates, in his own person, the world of the stage of years ago. The name of Nym comes from the Middle English *nimen,* "to take," and he is a thief. With Pistol, he separates Slender from his purse and Mistress Bridget from the handle of her fan. Nym's ubiquitous phrase, "That's my humour," betrays his origin.

Slender and Caius are excellent comic roles. As unsuccessful wooers to Anne Page, they have an integral function in the plot. Their origins lie in the two grotesques frequently found as unsuc-cesful suitors to the *amorosa* in Italian comedy — a duo Shakespeare has already used in *The Shrew.* In *The Merry Wives,* he emphasizes one characteristic each (like both humours and farci-cal figures), but in the playing there is more to them than that.

The actor of Caius begins as a choleric Frenchman, anoth-er version of "Il Dottore" of the *commedia;* but he discovers twists in the character that are almost as rich as Goldoni's alter-ations to the doctor figure, which did not begin until "the Great Season" of 1750. In making Caius a French physician, Shakespeare was probably mocking upper-class Londoners for using foreign physicians — a connection with the *commedia* tradition, a constant source for Shakespearean comedy, of making foreigners ridiculous. On stage, Caius is very funny. He has pugnacity (often expressed in his favourite oath, "by gar") and tears up the English language with Gallic abandon. His final threat "by gar, I'll raise all Windsor" (V.v.203-204) need not be performed as an empty threat: it has a similar force to Malvolio's "I'll be revenged on the whole pack of you" at the close of *Twelfth Night*. In Shakespeare's comedies we are often reminded that Elizabethans poked fun at the expense of one person, like those who aspire to the hands of unobtainable women (e.g., Malvolio, Falstaff) and risk being treated as fools. They must accept their "put down" by others.

In contrast, Slender is played as a rural gull — a character common to comedy in all ages. He no sooner arrives in Windsor than he is robbed by Pistol, Nym, and Bardolph. In the suit to Anne Page, Slender is passive and utterly without initiative: "I had rather than forty shillings I had my Book of Songs and Sonnets here" (I.i.183-184). But the actor must not allow the audience to sorrow over Slender. Shakespeare's intentions are clear; Slender is one of the finest comic portraits Shakespeare achieved in such little time and space. With incredible mastery and the most delicate touches, he makes the audience feel warmly toward Slender. We feel *for* him — and it is the actor's task to achieve this effect. Not only does Slender's intellect flicker with its last feeble glimmer, but his will has almost disappeared; he clings for support to Shallow. Slender's knowledge is confined to bears and greyhounds. His courage is not strong enough to stand up to the bluster of Pistol and Bardolph. Although Evans tries patiently to explain to him the "matter" of the wooing of Anne Page, "if you be capacity of it" (I.i.220), he has no capacity, and his enthusiasm rises only to, "Why, if it be so, I will marry her upon any reasonable demands ... that I am freely dissolved, and dissolutely" (I.i.209-234). Hilariously, he wanders through one scene (III.iv) doing nothing but sigh, quite irrelevantly, "O sweet Anne Page!" — unsuccessfully playing the part of the love-sick swain.

The nearest character to a humours portrait in *The Merry Wives* is Ford. All Windsor knows, as Quickly quickly relates, that "he's a very jealousy man" (II.ii.86-87). Ford openly talks

of jealousy, and in private he shows he is so consumed by jealousy that he would

> rather trust a Fleming with my butter, Parson Hugh the
> Welshman with my cheese, an Irishman with my aqua-
> vitae bottle, or a thief to walk my ambling gelding, than
> my wife with herself ... God be praised for my jealousy!
>   (II.ii.287-294)

Ford's passion is so intense that he becomes jealous enough to
hire another man, Falstaff, to seduce his wife — a typical plot
from the Italian Renaissance. In Elizabethan comedy, jealousy
is usually shown as a "humour" which dominates a man's character and leaves no room for other aspects of his temperament.
But the actor in the role must depict Ford's jealousy in three
dimensions; he must show that a man may be jealous and still
not be beneath contempt. Ford convinces himself that he
would be foolish not to be jealous — that jealousy is a risk
worth taking because his alternative is not to acknowledge
what might happen. He thinks:

> Though Page be a secure fool and stands so firmly on
> his wife's frailty, yet I cannot put off my opinion so easi-
> ly. She was in his company at Page's house, and what
> they made there I know not. Well, I will look further
> into't, and I have a disguise to sound Falstaff. If I find
> her honest, I lose not my labour. If she be otherwise,
> 'tis labour well bestowed.   (II.i.215-221)

The performer should be aware that, as Brook, it is in character
for Ford to continue to torture himself by hearing of Falstaff's
hopes and fictional progress. The actor can gently hint at a strain
of masochism, but no more than hint. Then, at the proper
moment Ford sees the foolishness of his ways and repents (IV.iv).

Page is a less rewarding role. He is little more than an aver-
age decent citizen; above suspecting his wife, he is not above
choosing his daughter's husband. Thus he must be gulled: he
discovers that his daughter is independent enough to run off
with the man she wants, and so she escapes the fool to whom
her father would rashly have married her.

The role of Fenton appears to be the youthful romantic
lead. But he is saved from the usual blandness of such characters because he kept company with the wild Prince and Poins,
and through his dignity and his willingness to act in the face of

the difficulties that beset his wooing. He also gains by contrast with his rivals — a common dramatic device — for the hand of Anne, in this case because he is poor yet of a higher class than Anne Page.

Shallow, who is one of Shakespeare's greatest creations in *2 Henry IV,* has no real function in *The Merry Wives* and wanders in and out. Yet the humour of this role for the player is varied. He remains the talkative, empty-headed country justice, but the fun of him comes largely from his vanity — particularly as that depends, as in *2 Henry IV,* on three factors. First, he has unreliable memories of his prowess when he was young. Second, he repeats the most trivial of phrases: "He hath wronged me, indeed he hath, at a word, he hath. Believe me — Robert Shallow, Esquire, saith he is wronged" (I.i.99-101). And third, he is unable either to avoid a platitude or to strike the right tone with a remark: "Though we are justices and doctors and churchmen, Master Page, we have some salt of our youth in us. We are the sons of women, Master Page" (II.iii.42-44).

The Welsh parson, Hugh Evans, is in the play to "make fritters of English" and, with his cowardice and over-anxious good nature, to serve also as a foil to his original foe and later collaborator, Caius. Played well, he is unforgettable in the Latin lesson. Shakespeare capitalizes on the interest in stage Welshmen which started about 1593 and continued for several years — as with Glendower and Fluellen in Shakespeare's other plays. All are of the same period, so perhaps Shakespeare's company had a specialist in Welsh roles. And in this play, the memorable moment of "that Welsh fairy" remains with us long after we have left the theatre.

Caius' "dry nurse," Mistress Quickly, also murders the English language and has even less control over her tongue: her thoughts pour out in verbal chaos. Together with the jovial bluster of the Host and the comic mistakes of the young page, they make one of the most astonishing groups of creators of fun and joy that even Shakespeare ever put in a play.

VERSE AND PROSE

Most of the play is in prose, and so a flowing colloquial effect is sustained on stage. The occasional modulation into verse is not as abrupt as has sometimes been maintained: it is nearly always associated either with Fenton, to identify the romantic subplot, or with the Herne the Hunter masque, as a sign of its fictional reality.

The Merry Wives does not have the intensity for commanding metaphors. Yet there are five major clusters of images that influence the audience's reaction to the story, the characters, and the atmosphere:

[1]   Domestic family life in a country town: e.g., "half stewed in grease like a Dutch dish."

[2]   The outdoors: e.g., "these lisping hawthorn-buds" and "he smells April and May."

[3]   Animals and birds: e.g., "like rats" and "unkennel the fox."

[4]   Falstaff's bulk (as in *1 & 2 Henry IV*). These images are used by him and of him. They commonly include those of oil, fat, and grease: e.g., "till the wicked fire of lust have melted him in his own grease" and "this whale, with so many tuns of oil in his belly," both from Mistress Ford.

[5]   The horns of the cuckold. These include a whole range of images related to bucks and other horned beasts. Ford fears that Falstaff is making him a cuckold, and Falstaff falsely thinks to make him one. These images culminate in that of Falstaff, wearing horns, awaiting the arrival of his "doe," at the beginning of the final scene. The extravagance of his "send me a cool rut-time, Jove" makes him ridiculous.

In this middle-class context, most people speak appropriately in homely proverbs or choose their allusions from the better-known parts of scripture, for example "The story of the Prodigal," "a legion of angels," and a "Cain-coloured beard." Classical allusions are naturally rare although several are used by the more highly educated Falstaff, and many have a sexual subtext.

CONCLUSION

The Merry Wives, in the Folio text, is the finest of all "citizen's comedies," a superb medley of all that would be likely to amuse an audience towards the close of the sixteenth century. It had a direct appeal to an aristocratic audience with its connections to the Queen and Windsor:

Cricket, to Windsor chimneys shalt thou leap.
Where fires thou findest unraked and hearths unswept,
There pinch the maids as blue as bilberry.
Our radiant Queen hates sluts and sluttery.   (V.v.43-46)

A few lines later the Fairy Queen instructs, "Search Windsor Castle, elves, within and out" (V.v.56). Two allusions to the Order of the Garter are strongly foregrounded: *Honi soit qui mal y pense* — the motto of the Order of the Garter — and the instructions to the fairies to scour "The several chairs of order" (V.v.61). These references remind us that earlier in the play (I.iv) Dr. Caius told us he was hurrying to court for a "grand affair." Also, Mistress Quickly noted that the town was filling with courtiers (II.ii). Clearly, something concerning the Order of the Garter is happening in Windsor.

The aristocratic audience was flattered by the assumption that it was educated, so Shakespeare includes the Latin scene (IV.i), which shows Quickly at her best. There are occasional witticisms of a literary kind, such as Parson Evans's confusion of a Marlowe lyric with a psalm, and the unromantic Falstaff accosting Mistress Ford, incongruously, with a line from Sir Philip Sidney's sonnet sequence Astrophel and Stella. As a "citizen's comedy," the play particularly appealed to the middle class, with a large farcical element directed to the groundlings.

In the theatre today, *The Merry Wives* appeals to everyone. Like so many other plays by Shakespeare, it is unique. There is no other play quite like it. That he writes, within the same brief number of years, his three major romantic comedies *(All's Well, As You Like It,* and *Twelfth Night),* is extraordinary. Shakespeare provides us with a remarkable range of love experiences: those of Beatrice and Benedick, Hero and Claudio, Rosalind and Orlando, Viola and Orsino, Olivia and Sebastian, Sir Toby and Maria, Anne Page and Fenton, Mistress Ford with Ford and Falstaff — what a wide display of human love interactions!

But when we reflect that, at the same time, Shakespeare also creates *1 & 2 Henry IV, Henry V, Julius Caesar,* and *Hamlet,* we can only be amazed at his genius.

CONCLUSION

LAUGHTER

uch Ado, As You Like It and *Twelfth Night* are, with *A Midsummer Night's Dream,* the greatest of Shakespeare's romantic comedies. Arguably they are as a group one of the greatest of human creations. These plays, like all romantic comedies, aim to interest the audience in a love story and to make them laugh.

What kind of laughter do these plays produce?

It is not the laughter of farce. Plays like *The Shrew* and *The Merry Wives* make the audience laugh in a different way from romantic comedy. Farce results in "belly laughs" at extreme comic action: for a hungry shrew to be deprived of food by her outrageous new husband, while he gently explains he is doing it for her own good, and for an old, fat, money-hungry and lecherous knight to be bundled up in a basket, as if he was dirty linen, do not produce subtle or delicate laughter.

The plays discussed in *Shakespeare's Comic World* show the variety in his early comedies. The audience's laughter changed from the "belly laughs" at the farce of *The Comedy of Errors* to amusement at the elegant wit of *Love's Labour's Lost;* from the happy wonder at the ethereal magic of *The Dream* to two kinds of laughter in *The Merchant of Venice* — the delight in the Belmont scenes and the near tragedy of those in Venice.

Much Ado, As You Like It and *Twelfth Night* are likely to make spectators smile and laugh warmly, amused by the love story and touched by the lovers in a way that is truly humorous. These plays are based on superb characters, people who are deeply drawn and who make the audience smile and chuckle. Beatrice and Benedick, Rosalind and Viola are delightful people we would be glad to meet any day; they are deeply in love and amuse us in their lovings. The gloriously warm humour conveyed by such people, who are caught in the sweetness and pangs of love, is one of Shakespeare's greatest achievements.

Yet, within the similarity of our laughter in Shakespeare's majestic middle comedies, there are some differences which the director must note. The audience at *As You Like It* feels continuous happiness, sheer joy in the inevitability of love. There are tangles and difficulties facing the hero and heroine, and even some dark forces in the play, but none of these disturb the audience's sense of well-being.

The audience at *Twelfth Night* would have slightly different feelings. They marvel at the unique world of Illyria and the charming people who inhabit it. But they are fully aware of the self-deception that fills the play, of how lovers can fool themselves in love. Thus *laughter at* Orsino, Olivia, Sir Andrew and Malvolio contrasts with *laughter with* Viola and Maria.

Much Ado, however, is different. We may *laugh at* the comic evil of Don John, and *laugh with* the wit of Beatrice and Benedick or the honest stupidities of Dogberry and the watch, but there are two extremes beyond these reactions. First is the absurdity of the non-existent thief, Deformed — as hilarious a creation as anything in the canon. Second is the mistreatment of Hero, at which the audience does not laugh: this is an ugly theme that contrasts with the rest of the play. Yet it also gives the comedy "bite": there is a tension between the feelings it evokes and the various kinds of laughter elsewhere in the play.

It is from the tensions in *Much Ado* that Shakespeare's later comedies emerge. In the three plays discussed in *Shakespeare's Problem World*, the comedy is so dark that the audience does not laugh very often. *All's Well That Ends Well*, *Measure for Measure* and *Troilus and Cressida* are dark and brooding. They leave a bitter taste after our laughter.

The Inigo Jones Theatre

Skin Market Tower

The Globe

Stage Machinery

Sculpture   Sculpture

Wishing Well

Sculptured Gates

Architect's drawing for the reconstruction of the Globe Theatre, Southwark, London, cut away to show the stage and heavens. The first plays will be staged during the Summer of 1995.

Project Architect:Theo Crosby, Pentagram Design, London.

END NOTES

ELIZABETHAN WORLD ORDER

Shakespeare's England is Christian. The English Reformation, begun by Henry VIII and continued by his daughter, Elizabeth I, establishes the Church of England (Anglican) as the official form of worship. But strong Catholic forces continue to work against the established church: the Armada, sent by Philip of Spain to restore Catholicism in England, is defeated in 1588, about the time Shakespeare arrives in London from Stratford-upon-Avon. Puritanism is also growing at this time.

Richard Hooker's great work defending the Anglican church, *Of the Laws of Ecclesiastical Polity,* says that God created the world according to a perfect plan. Each of his creations has a special function. As long as this order is preserved, the universe works beautifully and efficiently, with an orderly and permanent hierarchy, a chain of command from top to bottom. This chain is repeated in each realm of existence: thus God rules over the cosmos, the sun over the planets, the king over the body politic, the husband over the wife and family, the head over the other body parts, and so on. If this universal order is disturbed, chaos results — a great horror.

This view, derived from the male-oriented cultures of antiquity (Hittites, Israelites, Greeks, etc.), mixed with those aspects of Christianity encouraged by the Reformation.

The principle of order appears many times in Shakespeare's plays, most notably in Ulysses' speech on degree in *Troilus and Cressida* (I.iii.75-137) and Katherine's lecture to the other women on wifely submission at the end of *The Shrew* (V.ii.135-178) [see GENDER, below]. The breakdown of order is an offence against God: Macbeth's murder of Duncan, Paris's abduction of Helen from her lawful husband, the rejection of Lear by his daughters, Bolingbroke's overthrow of Richard II, and so on. The parallel of "king" to "sun" is used of Richard II, but not of Henry V because his father was a usurper, although Henry V is continually "golden."

PERSONALITY

A human being is a microcosm, a little world. His or her physical, mental and moral state resembles the macrocosm, somewhat like a hologram. The macrocosm can be seen as the body politic or as the universe. Both microcosm and macrocosm have four elements (fire, air, water, earth) which in people become four *humours:* blood, phlegm, yellow bile, and black bile. In Elizabethan psychology, they produce different "types" of people. These principles lie behind many comedies of the period (e.g., Ben Jonson's *Every Man in His Humour,* in which Shakespeare played a role), and they are inherent in many of Shakespeare's plays: e.g., Antony's final tribute to Brutus (*Julius Caesar,* V.v.68-75).

GENDER

Katherine's speech on wifely submission in *The Shrew* (V.ii.135-178) is a traditional Elizabethan view of the male-female relationship. This view is offensive to some modern feminists, but it must be understood in terms of Elizabethan mores. "Man" is the term used by Elizabethans for all human beings; females are clearly lesser beings. There is no reason to think that Shakespeare necessarily subscribed to this belief. It is true that throughout the plays he puts customary beliefs in the mouths of persons in the plays. Yet he often changes the traditional balance of males and females, particularly in the comedies, in which the woman may control the man (e.g., Helena, Rosalind) or be the focus of the action (Isabella, Portia). In this respect, Shakespeare is ahead of his contemporaries. Most of the tragedies, however, picture the female from the perspective of the male hero (e.g., Desdemona, Gertrude). The exception is *Antony and Cleopatra,* in which both have equal weight.

SOUL AND MIND

The Tudors use Aristotle's division of the soul into the vegetal, the sensible, and the rational faculties. The vegetal is shared by all living creatures and is responsible for the body's growth and generation. The sensible faculty, possessed by animals and people, is the source of feeling and motion. We perceive through the five senses. Perceptions are categorized by "the common sense," filtered through the imagination (fantasy), and ratified by reason.

Lack of imaginative control, as in illness, brings delusions. Delusions can also recur in sleep, when reason relaxes its vigilance, and Queen Mab gallops through the mind creating dreams (*Romeo & Juliet*, I.iv.53-103). Theseus in *The Dream* (V.i.4-22) shows that an unruly imagination is responsible for the erratic acts of lunatics, lovers, and poets. In this play the two pairs of lovers exemplify the delusions of unruly imagination.

TEXTS

The texts of Elizabethan dramatists were not exactly handled with care. The "Master of the Revels," a court official, examined each written script and often required moral or political revisions. The bookkeeper, or prompter, of the playhouse made the original manuscript (called "foul papers" or "fair copy") into a workable stage script (a "book") in which he wrote the cues, stage business, etc., together with any revisions or deletions made to satisfy the Master of the Revels. There were many such alterations, and sometimes the number of collaborators obscured the original author's intentions. Plays often remained in the repertory for a long time and could be revived periodically. Few plays were printed, because theatre managers were afraid that would reduce box-office receipts. Only forty or so of the two hundred or more plays performed between 1592 and 1603 have survived in print. Yet a reasonable reading public emerged for printed plays, usually in quarto editions.

Before 1623, nineteen of Shakespeare's plays had been published singly (in quarto), most more than once. Those printed from Shakespeare's own manuscripts, or from playhouse copies, are today called "good" quartos, while many "bad" quartos were pirated, often reconstructed from an actor's memory. *The First Folio*, in which Shakespeare's colleagues Hemmings and Condell collected most of his plays in one volume, was published in 1623 in a printing of about twelve hundred copies. It includes the engraving of Shakespeare by Martin Droeshout, a Flemish artist. This portrait is one of only two of Shakespeare known to be authentic; the other is the memorial bust in the Church of the Holy Trinity, Stratford.

SHAKESPEARE'S LANGUAGE

Elizabethan English is more flexible than the language of today. It has not settled down after its growth from Middle English into a modern form; it is not "fixed." For example, spelling is not uniform: the few existing examples of Shakespeare's signature show he even spells his name in different ways. He is not troubled by rigid rules of correctness, grammar, or definition. In addition to employing the common forms of his period, Shakespeare frequently uses language in his own distinctive way.

Elizabethan pronunciation is a matter of considerable scholarly debate. According to Kokeritz and others,* Shakespeare uses sounds similar to some modern English and American rural dialects: our *let* he pronounces *lit; virtue* as *vartue, nature* as *nater;* and *ea* like our *a* in t*ale,* so he said *speak* as *spake* and *dream* as *drame.* The noun *wind* could rhyme with either *kind* or *pinned.* Shakespeare sometimes makes two syllables of *-tion,* or adds a syllable to *Eng[e]land,* and at times makes a distinct syllable out of a final *-ed,* as in Antony's remark "The good is oft interrèd with their bones" (*Julius Caesar,* III.ii.77).

The verse basis of Shakespeare's plays is the iambic pentameter: iambic because there are two syllables with the accent on the second, and pentameter because there are five of them in a line, thus:

Te-TUM, te-TUM, te-TUM, te-TUM, te-TUM.

"And for I know she taketh most delight ... "
Shakespeare varies the beats in a line, and uses other line forms and prose, for dramatic effect. He uses rhyme more often in his early plays, to show artificiality, and can end a scene with a conventional rhyming couplet.

Renaissance writers have difficulty keeping pace with a language that is growing with the expansion of their social life. Shakespeare invents a vast range of words (e.g., assassination, disgraceful, gloomy, laughable, savagery) and combinations (e.g., falling to blows, an abrupt answer, bright and cheerful, sealing one's lips). More difficult for us are words that have changed their meaning or disappeared since Shakespeare used them. An example is "quibble," a game of "mis-taking the word": comic characters play it for fun, young lovers use it as a screen to hide their feelings

---

* See Kokeritz (1953) and Dobson (1968).

(like Beatrice and Benedick in *Much Ado*), and it can communicate simultaneously on two or more levels, often with irony.

G. Wilson Knight emphasizes that each Shakespeare play is "a visionary unit bound to obey none but its own self-imposed laws ... as an expanded metaphor, by means of which the original vision has been projected into forms roughly correspondent with actuality."[*] Apart from the time-sequence which is the story, each play is unified in space (the play's "atmosphere") through imagery. Shakespeare's images cluster in groups; thus there are many nature images, particularly those relating to growing things in gardens and orchards, and there are repeated images in individual plays — light and dark in *Romeo and Juliet*, disease in *Hamlet*, animals in action in *Othello*, and so on. But imagery almost always refers to the whole play and cannot be separated from other elements.

THE PLAYHOUSE

Shakespeare writes for performances in the Theatre, the Globe, and other specific buildings. Information about the playhouses is disappointingly scarce, so modern reconstructions have been mostly conjecture; recent archeological discoveries in London have provided little more data. But we know enough about the *principles* of the Elizabethan and Jacobean theatre spaces to understand *why*, *what*, and *how* things took place.

THE "HOUSE" AND THE "PLACE"
The Elizabethan stage evolved from earlier forms. The liturgical drama and the massive medieval Cycles were based on two acting-areas: the "house," a localized space (a Paradise, a Hell, an ark for Noah, etc.); and the "place," a generalized space in front of one or more "houses."

The arrangement differed with the position of the "houses": in a line on a stage, as at Valençiennes; around a town square, as at Lucerne; on wagons wheeled from "place" to "place" ("stations"), as with some English Cycles; or in a circle with the audience in the middle, as in the Cornish and other English Cycles. In all cases, much of the action happened in the "place."

Interlude and Morality plays were normally performed by small professional troupes in the lord's hall. There the screen provided

---

[*] Knight (1957) 14-15.

*Popular stage from ancient
times to Shakespeare's day:
"house" and "place"*

*Two kinds of "house" and "place" in a medieval performance in the
round*

*Interlude player in Tudor hall:
"house" is screen with two doors;
whole floor is "space"*

*Later adaptations to the medieval
hall: balcony at the top of the
screen; "tent" (curtains) set
against the centre of the screen*

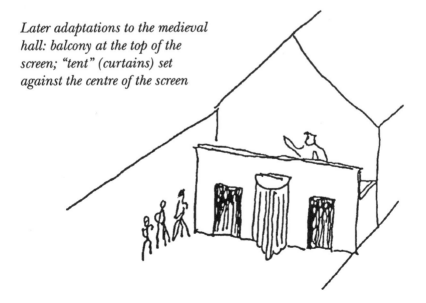

Conjectural Elizabethan playhouse (based on C. Walter Hodges); note the two doors and curtains for inner stage, plus upper stage, and trap door on the stage ("place")

an upper level, and on the ground level there were two doors on either side. On the wall between the doors was a "house" (sometimes a curtain) for entrances. The floor was the "place" where the actors performed. Single professional minstrels or small acting companies roamed far, performing in public streets, fields, taverns, and great houses. They set up the traditional booth stage of the old street theatre (a "house"), using any area around it as the "place."

In the sixteenth century, innyards were used. A wooden platform was built in the courtyard as a stage (the "place"), on which at least one "house" was probably sited. Spectators stood around, the stables became dressing rooms, and the several tiers of the gallery had seats for prosperous patrons. Some innkeepers in London and elsewhere found it profitable to lease their yards exclusively to theatrical companies. The playhouses used all these traditions, maintaining the localized "house" and the generalized "place."

THE PUBLIC PLAYHOUSES

In 1576 James Burbage built the Theatre, the first permanent playhouse in London, in the priory of Holywell, between Shoreditch High Street and Finsbury Fields. The site was just north of the city, outside the jurisdiction of the city authorities. In 1577 the Curtain was built nearby. In 1600 the manager, Philip Henslowe, with the actor Alleyn, built the Fortune, also to the north but west of Shoreditch. The Red Bull (c. 1605) was the last built to the north. An increasingly important area was Bankside, the south bank of the Thames, also beyond the control of the London council. On Bankside were built the Rose (c. 1587), the Swan (c. 1595), the Hope (1613), and in 1599 Burbage and his men transferred from the Theatre to the new Globe.

The professional companies were sponsored, but not financed, by prominent nobles. The Lord Chamberlain's Men owned and operated the Theatre and then the Globe; the company included Burbage, his son Richard, the famous actor, and Shakespeare. Their chief rival was the Lord Admiral's Men, managed by Henslowe. The principal actor of this company was Edward Alleyn, who created the role of Marlowe's Tamburlaine. The companies were continually harassed by the London burghers, who thought that the congregating mobs were a hazard to public health and law enforcement, and by Puritan agitators, like Stephen Gosson, who denounced theatres as inciting people to sin.

The open air Elizabethan playhouse was usually round or polygonal, although the Fortune may have been rectangular. James Burbage, whose Theatre was probably a model for the rest, had previously built bear-pits and may have been influenced by his experience.

The stage area was built on the principle of the "house" and the "place." A bare platform jutted out into an unroofed yard or pit. At the rear of the platform was part of the main building, called the tiring house which had two purposes. Within it, the actors dressed. But the wall that separated the tiring house from the spectators was the façade that backed the stage. This façade had two doors on either side for entries and exits. Between them was either a recess with a draw curtain or a "house," and above was a gallery *(tarras)* where high scenes could be played. Although this was much like the staging for interludes, over the stage area was a roof (the "heavens") for possible descents, for making the noise of thunder, and for protecting the actors from the weather. Under the stage was the hell, or cellarage, from which devils and ghosts could rise through a trapdoor. "You hear this fellow in the cellarage," Hamlet says when the Ghost speaks from below (I.v.151).

Scenery as we know it hardly existed. There were large and small stage properties — a throne for a king, a bed for Desdemona, a tree for Malvolio — which were brought in and out in front of the audience, or "revealed" as the rear curtain was drawn. Atmospheric scene changes were done with words:

> But look, the morn in russet mantle clad
> Walks o'er the dew of yon high eastward hill.
>
> *(Hamlet,* I.i.167-168)

Costuming was splendid, but there was little attempt at historical accuracy. The simplicity of the stage allowed the dramatic action to move forward swiftly and continuously and brought a physical closeness between actors and spectators, giving a special force to the aside and the soliloquy.

The groundlings stood in the pit. There were usually three tiers of gallery seats, which cost more. Gallants crowded onto the stage and might behave in a rowdy manner. The size of an Elizabethan audience averaged between two thousand and twenty five hundred. Johannes de Witt, a Dutch visitor who made the famous sketch of the Swan in 1596, said that it could seat three thousand, and there is no evidence to the contrary. Surrounded by gallants on the stage, groundlings in the pit, and the more affluent in the galleries, the actor appeared in the open air between the painted heavens above and the hell below.

THE "PRIVATE" THEATRES

Plays were also presented at the "private" theatres, often rented halls where more aristocratic artistic and moral traditions existed. Anyone could attend, but they catered to a small affluent group. These halls were roofed, well heated, and artificially lit, so they could be used in bad weather and at night.

Most housed troupes of children. Several London choir schools trained boys into expert actors in their own troupes; they were exploited on the commercial stage. These child troupes are not to be confused with the individual professional boy actors who took female roles in the adult troupes performing in the public playhouses.

When Hamlet asks why the players visiting Elsinore have left the city, Rosencrantz says they are victims of a "late innovation" (II.ii.332) of child troupes that has hurt their business:

> But there is, sir, an eyrie [nest] of children, little eyas-
> es [hawk chicks], that cry out on the top of question
> and are most tyrannically clapped for't. These are now
> the fashion, and so berattle the common stages — so
> they call them — that many wearing rapiers are afraid
> of goose quills and dare scarce come thither.
> *(Hamlet,* II.ii.338-343)

That is, many Londoners did not attend the "private" theatres in case they were satirized by dramatists writing for the children's companies. Shakespeare's company gave winter performances in Blackfriars, a "private" theatre, after 1608.

THE DRAMATIC WORLD

"All the world's a stage," says Jaques. The comparison of the world with the stage, the *theatrum mundi,* runs throughout Shakespeare's works. He uses it in a variety of ways, changing its meaning from play to play. Although he did not invent the concept, he made it particularly his own.

DOUBLE MEANINGS

The "theatre of the world," the ancient play metaphor, is of great antiquity: it is used by Pythagoras, Plato, and Augustus Caesar; it occurs in Menander's *The Arbitrants,* and in Plautus and Terence, where characters, and by implication the audience, accept the *play world* as reality.*

In medieval England, the metaphor is used mostly in non-dramatic literature, as with Wyclif. Only in the sixteenth century, when the morality play becomes secular, do dramatists use the metaphor (based on Prudentius' *Psychomachia*) that acting is a disguise: the evil people in Skelton and Lyndsay change their names and clothes to seem honourable to their victims. Once actors are seen as dissemblers confusing honest men with illusion, comments about playing the "knave," or the "part," have a new and sinister quality. John Bale's play, *Kyng Johan* (c. 1539), is full of multiple changes of deceit.

The Vice survives on the Tudor secular stage. In early moralities he is a popular, accomplished rascal, a witty schemer, and a manipulator of the plot. He speaks to the onlookers using questions, insults, and mocking offers, which amuses them and keeps their attention. This brilliant figure joins "actor" to "deceiver," a double meaning taken up by the Puritans who see actors as hypocrites and counterfeits, people who persuade honest men of lies using names and costumes not their own. The Vice's audience address preserves the link between the players and the spectators. Play images cluster to him: in Heywood's *Play of Love* (c. 1532), the Vice pretends love for a woman he knows to be false; in *Ralph Roister Doister* (c. 1550), Merygreeke and Custance plan to gull the braggart by devising a playlet as a dramatist might plan a play; and Diccon, the Vice in *Gammer Gurton's Needle* (c. 1560), makes his mischievous plots dramatic.

Although the aside remains, the Vice's audience address and his clowning make his position in the play ambiguous, particularly when other people cannot overhear him. The final secularization of the theatre and the growth of the play as illusion allow the dramatic metaphor to enter English drama. In Gascoigne's play, *The Supposes* (1566), a character is astonished by a twist to the plot and suggests that "a man might make a Comedie of it" (V.vii.61-62). John Lyly's comedies, performed at court, no longer use the audience address, but prologues emphasize the dream-like nature of the play; the Prologue of *Sapho and Phao* (1584) asks the Queen to wake at the end of the performance. These traditions Shakespeare inherits.

---

* For references, see Righter (repr. 1967).

THE PLAY-WITHIN-THE-PLAY

The recognition of the theatrical nature of life originated in the medieval tradition and took form between 1550 and the work of Thomas Kyd, when the play establishes itself as illusion. Kyd's *The Spanish Tragedy* (c. 1589) deliberately builds on the metaphor of the world as a stage and creates "the play-within-the-play." Until then, experiments with this device were limited to *Fulgens and Lucres* and the anonymous *Rare Triumphs of Love and Fortune* (c. 1582). Kyd unites the medieval contact with the audience to the device of the self-sufficient play; but he does not use audience address. He relies on "the play-within-the-play" so extensively that the actual audience faces an image of itself: actors who sit as spectators within the play (actual vs. fictional; real Londoners vs. the imaginary court of Spain). This perspective becomes a major device of the time, and Shakespeare relies upon it.

When plays are first given in the new Theatre, the direct link of the audience and stage personages is renewed. Bridges between the real world (audience) and the *play world* are given by prologues, epilogues, and Chorus speeches, while within the play's action a bridge is provided by the aside and dramatic monologues. The audience address becomes the soliloquy; conventionally overheard by the spectators, it is not necessarily directed to them. For over half a century the soliloquy implies a deliberately vague relation of audience to personage, spectator to actor.

Many believe in the power that illusion has over reality. Hamlet says,

The play's the thing
Wherein I'll catch the conscience of the king.

(II.ii.602-603)

This belief in the power of illusion is basic to the new relation between actors and audience and to the effectiveness of the play metaphor. It could change people's lives. This belief continues with other dramatists: the citizen's wife of *The Knight of the Burning Pestle* (1607) and Jonson's poor gull in *Bartholomew Fair* (1614) are aware that the play they watch is only shadows, but then they forget. The play holds a mirror up to nature; it reflects the reality of its audience. But illusion affects the audience in many ways: some mistake illusion for reality, while others use the language and gestures of the theatre in the actual world.

THE METAPHOR IN SHAKESPEARE

Shakespeare combines direct and indirect references to the audience (e.g., *1 Henry IV,* V.iv.124-125; *Measure for Measure,* II.iv.9-10; *The Dream,* II.i.223-226) with the metaphor of the "theatre of the world." Shakespeare's play metaphors work in three related ways: they express the depth of the *play world;* they define the relation of that world to the actual world of the audience; and they show the illusion of ordinary life.

The association of the world with the stage builds itself deeply into his imagination and the structure of his plays. He uses play metaphors to a degree unusual even among his contemporaries.

Allied to the play metaphor is the use of boys for women's parts. In *Twelfth Night* and *As You Like It,* boys play the parts of girls who are acting the roles of boys. Rosalind is very conscious of this inversion, and Viola gently reminds us of gender differences.

A number of Shakespeare's characters function as dramatists within a play; they follow a dramatic plan towards a desired end. They differ in how they do so in two broad types, the actor-dramatist and the director-dramatist, those who act out their own dramatizations and those who manipulate others to perform events, as follows:

- *The actor-dramatist:* The actor-dramatist devises and acts out his own imagined dramas either because of self-delusion (Orsino) or in order to establish his bearings in a vast and chaotic universe (Lear).

  The actor-dramatist may include others in his own dramas, but he almost never forces them to play a part. Petruchio, for example, acts upon the rest of the characters as an actor-dramatist but acts as a director-dramatist when he manipulates Katherine. Othello is more extreme when he makes Desdemona fit into his drama by killing her.

- *The director-dramatist:* The director-dramatist knows what he is doing; he always has a firm goal. This kind of person plots with care before he acts, but, like Iago or Richard III, he often does so only one scene at a time. He functions with equal ease in comedy and tragedy and is related to the Vice, the clever slave servant of classical comedy, and the stage Machiavel. The most extreme kind, like Richard III, is a puppet master. The usual climax of his play is when he compels his victim to accept a new role. He is sometimes a subordinate character who initiates things or keeps them moving, bringing about the comic or tragic sufferings of the protagonists, as Pandarus and Sir Toby. But in *Richard III, Measure for Measure,* and *The Tempest,* he is the protagonist.

THE PLAYER KING

Queen Elizabeth I said that monarchs, like actors, stand on a stage in the sight of all the world, and the least blemish is visible to both enemies and friends. Shakespeare knew that the actual king sees in the player's performance an aspect of kingship itself. Then the juxtaposition of illusion and reality is enormously powerful and complex. The king at his coronation assumes a dramatic role, a part which he must interpret, but which he may not fundamentally change (Richard III cannot cope with this task). A king is identified with his dramatic role; he cannot be separated from it except by death or violence. He is the timeless and ideal symbol of things, the deputy of God on earth, the representative of the land and a people. He is a paradox: a particular person; and the embodiment of an abstract ideal. The pomp and ceremony that surround him are not an idle show; they distance him from the common reality, and they are the outward expression of authority. Form, tradition, ritual, dress, and procession make kingship visible.

The actor who plays the king is a greater paradox: he is a person and a player in the role of a king. In the trappings of royalty, he is a "mock king," like the ancient Whitsun monarch or Lord of Misrule. The Player King is a private man who sees his royalty as dream-like and insubstantial. When he takes off his crown and robes he is separated from his splendour and becomes "ordinary" again. In the history plays the Player King mechanically acts out the gestures of a role for which he is not suited (Henry VI, Richard III, Richard II, John), and he confronts an opposite who aspires to his role and who often helps his cause through the use of conscious role-playing (e.g., Richard Duke of York, Richard of Gloucester, Richmond, Bolingbroke, Faulconbridge).

THE PLAY AS DREAM

Shakespeare asks the audience to accept that the play is as important in their lives as their own dreams. He often uses "dream" and "play" synonymously; both are illusions. But as people in actual and fictional worlds have dreams, "dream" is a third reality distinct from those in which the audience and players live.

Dreams originate either inside or outside a person's consciousness and can be of natural, diabolical, or divine origin.
Sceptics think that dreams have natural, internal causes and do
not foretell the future. A dream is caused by a disturbance in the
imagination: the bodily spirits of the senses retain some images
when they return to the heart, or brain, during sleep; they offer
images to the imaginative faculty and produce dreams. According
to George Chapman, imagination can be

> stirr'd up by forms in the memory's store,
> Or by the vapours of o'erflowing humours.
>
> (*The Revenge of Bussy d'Ambois*, V.i.44-45)

Any disturbances in the normal balance of the bodily humours,
the mind, indigestion, hunger, nervousness, or fear affect the
imagination and are released in dream. Or, says Tourneur, dreams
might be caused by

> the raised
> Impressions of premeditated things,
> By serious apprehension left upon
> Our minds.   (*The Atheist's Tragedy*, II.vi.29-32)

Hamlet calls dreams "a shadow" (II.ii.69), and Hastings, in *Richard
III*, insists they are "the mockery of unquiet slumbers" (III.ii.27).
Romeo says that dreamers "do dream things true" (I.iv.52), but
Mercutio answers with his Queen Mab speech; dreams, he says,
reveal the wishes of the dreamer. They

> are the children of an idle brain,
> Begot of nothing but vain fantasy ...
>
> (*Romeo & Juliet*, I.iv.97-98)

Imagination provides the dream with content, which consists of
the events and worries of the actual world. It is memory more
than fear or anguish that causes Lady Macbeth to sleepwalk.
Richard III's dreams can be thought natural (they originate in
Richard's memory), or divine (he is God's agent), or diabolical
and supernatural (he is a devilish villain).

For Shakespeare, both malign and benign spirits exist. The
malign are "objective evil": spirits, witches, ghosts, devils, demons,
who project their power into nature and influence us but cannot
change free will. They affect us from without, when they offer us a
physical but insubstantial object (as evil spirits offer Macbeth a dagger); or from within, when they interfere with the humours to
affect our senses. Dreams from spirits can lead us either to damnation or salvation. If benign, dreams warn us of future events. If

malign, they delude us by playing on our desires — they deceive our imagination, fog our reason, and lead us to destruction. Shakespeare is ambivalent about the origin of dreams. He knows spirits exist, and that they affect the universe in storms (as in *The Tempest*), in dreams (as in *Richard III*), or are a mode of communication between the real and the spirit worlds (as in *Hamlet*). People respond to dreams of their own free will. Hamlet and Macbeth are free to accept or reject the advice given in dream. Yet Shakespeare also knows that dreams of any origin are produced by the imagination, and no matter how real they seem, they are illusory.

Shakespeare consistently shows that, when people respond to dreams, their character is revealed by their choice. In the actual world, the *play world*, or the dream world, the individual's response to events tells us of his or her character. Lucullus, in *Timon of Athens*, and Shylock, in *The Merchant of Venice*, are the kind of people who would dream of riches, and they do, but their responses differ. Julius Caesar and Hector respond to their wives' dreams similarly. For Shakespeare, the dream is an imaginative reality. But who we are, and what we do in the actual world can affect our dreams: Hermia wakes up screaming in *The Dream* (II.ii.151-156); Katharine of Aragon, in *Henry VIII*, dreams a masque and responds in sleep with "signs of rejoicing"; and Richard III at Bosworth cries out in the actual world his dream-fears — "Give me another horse! Bind up my wounds! Have mercy, Jesu!" (V.iii.178-179) — that

> Have struck more terror to the soul of Richard
> Than can the substance of ten thousand soldiers ...
> (V.iii.218-219)

Dream may affect us in the actual world for any length of time: Christopher Sly, in *The Shrew*, thinks he has been in a dream for fifteen years; he sees his actual experience as dream. Richard II (V.i.18) and Katharine of Aragon (*Henry VIII*, II.iv.71) use dreams to cover a long period of happy time; and they wake to an unpleasant actuality. Similarly Henry V spurns Falstaff:

> I know thee not, old man. Fall to thy prayers.
> How ill white hairs becomes a fool and jester.
> I have long dreamt of such a kind of man,
> So surfeit-swelled, so old, and so profane,
> But being awaked I do despise my dream.
> (*2 Henry IV*, V.v.50-54)

His early adventures with Falstaff are now "my dream" (unreal and insubstantial), and he wakes to the actuality of kingship. This constant interchange of actual to dream, and vice versa, shows their vague boundaries.

Shakespeare thinks of the relation of the *play world* and the actual world much like the relation of the dream world and the *play world*. Hamlet equates the actor's art, and the world that art creates, with dream (II.ii.549); and Theseus says the play as a whole is a dream — "The best in this kind are but shadows; and the worst are no worse, if imagination amend them" *(The Dream,* V.i.208-209). Both figures in dreams and people in a play are shadows. Macbeth says,

> Life's but a walking shadow, a poor player
> That struts and frets his hour upon the stage
> And then is heard no more.   (V.v.24-26)

The imagination bridges gaps between "worlds." The poet works imaginatively (as Theseus says) and has this faculty more than others. *Henry V* overcomes the gap between the actual world and the *play world* by prologues in which the Chorus constantly asks the audience to let the players "On your imaginary forces work" (I.Pro.18).

Shakespeare insists on the play's relevance to the lives of the spectators. He says it is a dream designed by the playwright, and the actor is the manipulator of that dream. It is then imaginatively re-created in the actual world by the audience.

The audience must understand that the play is not distinctly different from the actual world. A great play is not just to be enjoyed and forgotten but is a profound imaginative reality as relevant to their lives as their own dreams.

THE TUDOR MYTH

Elizabeth I was the granddaughter of Henry VII (Henry Tudor), the founder of the Tudor dynasty. As his claim to the throne was weak, two themes of the developing Tudor myth emphasized specific aspects of history. First, Henry VII claimed to be descended from King Arthur, fulfilling the prophecies of Cadwallader, last of the Briton kings — a story told by Leland and other chroniclers and in Spenser's *Faerie Queene.* But second, Henry VII won the right to the crown at Bosworth, which also ended the tragic Lancaster-York feud in the Wars of the Roses.

This story was told by three main chroniclers: Polydore Vergil, Edward Hall, and Raphael Holinshed, who saw the Wars as a pattern of cause-and-effect, murder-and-revenge, sin-and-punishment. England's guilt, which came about when Bolingbroke usurped the crown from the true king, Richard II, is transmitted down the generations (as in Aeschylean tragedy) until it is expiated at Bosworth where Richmond, before he kills Richard III, prays and sees himself as an agent of God's justice:

> O Thou, whose captain I account myself,
> Look on my forces with a gracious eye;
> Put in their hands Thy bruising irons of wrath,
> That they may crush down with a heavy fall
> Th'usurping helmets of our adversaries;
> Make us Thy ministers of chastisement,
> That we may praise Thee in the victory.
> (*Richard III,* V.iii.109-115)

But Shakespeare tackles this civil strife in a peculiar order. He writes the plays about the last half first. It is only in the middle of the 1590s that he begins at the beginning. Richard II is the true but weak king who is overthrown by Bolingbroke of Lancaster in 1399; thus England is cursed by God to suffer until the rightful king is crowned. The reigns of Bolingbroke, as Henry IV, and his son, Henry V, follow.

Shakespeare began his early English histories with Henry V's death (1422). The young, weak son of Henry V, Henry VI, after years of factionalism and turbulence, is overthrown by the Yorkists: Edward II and then his brother, the villainous Richard III, killed at Bosworth by Henry Tudor in 1485.

For the Tudors, the break with the medieval line of succession when Richard II is deposed began an era of political disorder. Would a similar disorder happen on Elizabeth's death? Shakespeare focuses on the *role* of king — on the *symbol* of the crown — and he stresses its external theatricality. Henry VI uses it weakly, Richard III wickedly, so that the four early plays are one long tragedy: of England's collapse; of the people who fall; and of a role that no one can fill. The further away we are from Tudor times, the less the audience knows about the historical facts. But these are not of primary importance. Shakespeare sacrifices historical accuracy for dramatic effect to present us with enthralling people.

Each of the eight sequential plays of English history is a single unit. But created by one imagination, they make a coherent whole, often called epic in character — perhaps the only modern work that can be compared to Homer's epics. It has been said that its focus is not a single person but England: the decline and fall of the Plantagenets, with a prologue about King John and an epilogue on Henry VIII. The historical order of the reigns is less relevant to Shakespeare's imagination than the symbolic order. The plays begin with the greatest political confusion and national weakness under Richard II and end after a great victory by a national hero (Henry VII).

There are differences in quality: only *Richard III* among the early histories compares with the glories of Shakespeare's second group. They have different structures; for each play he creates a new structure to fit a unique historical and political context. There is, for instance, a radical change with *Richard III:* a tighter structure is dominated by a magnetic person, and a whole new idea of the history play comes into being.

Nor does Shakespeare swallow the Tudor myth whole. He accepts the most important issue: Richmond's victory meant that God chose the Tudor monarchs to be his exalted deputies on earth, so obedience to the king is obedience to God. This Shakespeare re-creates as the principle of order in Ulysses' speech on degree *(Troilus and Cressida,* I.iii.75-137), and it is believed by Faulconbridge in *King John* and Richmond in *Richard III.*

But Shakespeare does not accept it completely. His histories have ambiguities, irony, and a dialogic process. His are not plays with "a message," that uncritically put forward specific moral ideas — Shakespeare in the histories is ambivalent about many ideas. His intuition goes beyond the morality of the Tudor myth to question it with sly, subtle ambiguities and even cast doubts on its human truth. He is writing not history but plays for the living stage. His success is evident when we see them today.

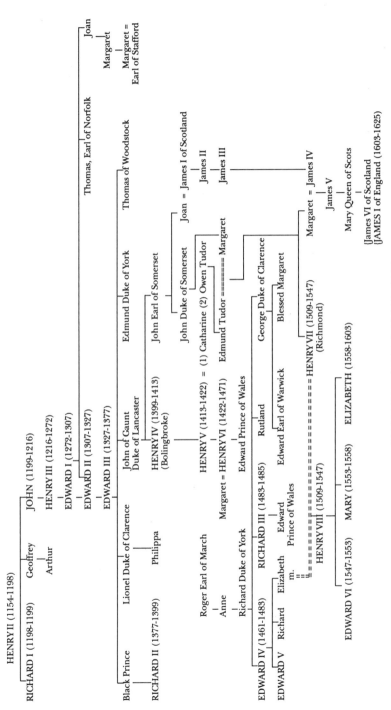

ENGLISH MONARCHS 1154-1625

William Shakespeare was born in 1564 to a prosperous middle-class family in Stratford on Avon. By the age of thirty he was already well established in the London theatre scene. Around 1610 he retired to Stratford, where he died in 1616. The chronology below gives approximate dates the plays were written. From about 1588 to 1600 he wrote mainly history plays and comedies; from 1600 to 1608 tragedies and "dark" comedies, and from 1608 to 1612 dramatic romances.

Chronology of the Plays:

1588-1591	*2 Henry VI, 3 Henry VI*
1588-1594	*The Comedy of Errors, Love's Labour's Lost*
1590-1592	*1 Henry VI*
1590-1594	*Titus Andronicus, King John*
1592-1593	*Richard III*
1593-1594	*The Taming of the Shrew*
1593-1595	*The Two Gentlemen of Verona*
1594-1596	*Romeo and Juliet, A Midsummer Night's Dream*
1593-1595	*Richard II*
1594-1597	*The Merchant of Venice*
1597	*1 Henry IV*
1597-1598	*2 Henry IV*
1597-1601	*The Merry Wives of Windsor*
1598-1599	*Henry V*
1597-1600	*Much Ado About Nothing*
1599	*Julius Caesar*
1599-1600	*As You Like It, Twelfth Night*
1600-1601	*Hamlet*
1601-1602	*Troilus and Cressida*
1602-1604	*All's Well That Ends Well*
1602-1604	*Othello, Measure for Measure*
1604-1606	*King Lear, Macbeth*
1604-1608	*Timon of Athens*
1605-1607	*Antony and Cleopatra*
1606-1609	*Coriolanus*
1608-1609	*Pericles*
1609-1610	*Cymbeline*
1610-1611	*The Winter's Tale*
1611	*The Tempest*
1612-1613	*Henry VIII, Two Noble Kinsmen*

WORKS RECOMMENDED
FOR STUDY
—— ALL VOLUMES ——

Beckerman, Bernard. *Shakespeare at the Globe 1599-1609*. London: Collier-Macmillan, 1962.

Bevington, David. *Action is Eloquence*. Cambridge: Harvard University Press, 1984.

Boas, F. S. *Shakespere and His Predecessors*. New York: Haskell House [1896], repr. 1968.

Bradbrook, Muriel C. *Shakespeare: The Poet in his World*. New York: Columbia University Press, 1978.

Bullough, Geoffrey. *Narrative and Dramatic Sources of Shakespeare*. 8 vols. New York: Columbia University Press, 1957-1975.

Calderwood, James L. *Shakespearean Metadrama*. Minneapolis: University of Minnesota Press, 1971.

Courtney, Richard. *Outline History of British Drama*. Totawa, N. J.: Littlefield, Adams, & Co., 1982.

Dollimore, Jonathan. *Radical Tragedy*. Chicago: University of Chicago Press, 1986.

Dollimore, Jonathan, and Alan Sinfield, eds. *Political Shakespeare*. Ithaca, N.Y.: Cornell University Press, 1985.

Ford, Boris, ed. *The Age of Shakespeare*. London: Cassell, 1961.

Frye, Northrop. *A Natural Perspective: The Development of Shakespearean Comedy and Romance*. New York: Columbia University Press, 1965.

—. *Fools of Time: Studies in Shakespearean Tragedy*. Toronto: University of Toronto Press, 1967.

—. *The Myth of Deliverance*. Toronto: University of Toronto Press, 1984.

—. *Northrop Frye on Shakespeare*. Toronto: Fitzhenry & Whiteside, 1986.

Gaster, T. H. *Thespis: Ritual, Myth and Drama in the Ancient Near-East*. New York: Doubleday, 2nd rev. ed., 1961.

Granville-Barker, Harley. *Prefaces to Shakespeare*. 4 vols. London: Batsford, repr. 1963.

Greenblatt, Stephen. *Renaissance Self-Fashioning*. Chicago: University of Chicago Press, 1980.

—. *Shakespearean Negotiations*. Berkeley and Los Angeles: University of California Press, 1988.

—. *Learning to Curse*. London: Routledge, 1990.

Howard, Jean E., and Marion F. O'Connor, eds. *Shakespeare Reproduced*. London: Methuen, 1987.

Kastan, David Scott, and Peter Stallybrass. *Staging the Renaissance.* London: Routledge, 1991.

Kinney, Arthur F., and Dan S. Collins, eds. *Renaissance Historicism.* Boston: University of Massachusetts, 1987.

Knight, G. Wilson. *Shakespearean Production.* London: Faber, 1964.

—. *Shakespeare and Religion.* London: Routledge and Kegan Paul, 1967.

Kott, Jan. *Shakespeare Our Contemporary.* Trans. B. Taborski. New York: Doubleday [1964], rev. 1967.

Leggatt, Alexander. *Shakespeare's Political Drama.* London: Routledge, 1988.

McGuire, Philip C., and David A. Samuelson. *Shakespeare: The Theatrical Dimension.* Washington: AMS Foundation, 1979.

Muir, Kenneth. *Shakespeare's Sources.* London: Methuen, 1957.

—. *Shakespeare the Professional.* Totawa, N. J.: Littlefield, Adams, & Co., 1973.

Nagler, A. M. *Shakespeare's Stage.* Trans. Ralph Manheim. New Haven: Yale University Press, 1958.

Oxford Companion to the Theatre and *Oxford Companion to the Canadian Theatre.* Toronto: Oxford University Press.

Righter, Anne. *Shakespeare and the Idea of the Play.* Harmondsworth: Penguin [1967], repr. 1982.

Salgado, Gamini. *Eyewitnesses to Shakespeare: First Hand Accounts of Performances 1590-1890.* London: Chatto & Windus, 1975.

Sinfield, Alan. *Faultlines.* Trans. Ralph Manheim. Berkeley and Los Angeles: University of California, 1992.

Slater, Ann Pasternak. *Shakespeare the Director.* New York: Barnes & Noble, 1982.

Sprague, Arthur Colby. *Shakespeare and the Actors.* Cambridge: Harvard University Press, 1944.

—. *Shakespearean Players and Performances.* Cambridge: Harvard University Press, 1953.

Sprague, Arthur Colby, and J. C. Trewin. *Shakespeare's Plays Today: Some Customs and Conventions of the Stage.* London: Sidgwick and Jackson, 1970.

Styan, J.L. *The Shakespeare Revolution.* Cambridge: Cambridge University Press, 1977.

Thomas, Brook. *New Historicism and Other Old-Fashioned Topics.* Princeton: Princeton University Press, 1991.

Van Laan, Thomas F. *Role-Playing in Shakespeare.* Toronto: University of Toronto Press, 1978.

Veeser, Aram, ed. *The New Historicism.* London: Routledge, 1989.

Wells, Stanley. *The Cambridge Companion to Shakespeare Studies.* Cambridge: Cambridge University Press, 1986.

Zesmer, David A. *Guide to Shakespeare.* New York: Barnes and Noble, 1976.

—— THE MIDDLE COMEDIES ——

Barber, C. L. *Shakespeare's Festive-Comedy*. Princeton: Princeton University
Press, 1959.

Barnet, Sylvan. "*As You Like It* on Stage." In *As You Like It*, 238-250. New York:
Signet [1963], 1987.

Barnet, Sylvan. "*Twelfth Night* on Stage." In *Twelfth Night*, 215-225. New York:
Signet, 1965.

Bradbrook, M. C. *The Growth and Structure of Elizabethan Comedy*. London:
Chatto & Windus, 1955.

Brown, John Russell, and Bernard Harris, eds. *Early Shakespeare*. London:
Edward Arnold, 1961.

Champion, Larry S. *The Evolution of Shakespeare's Comedy*. Cambridge: Harvard
University Press, 1970.

Frye, Northrop. "The Argument of Comedy." In *English Institute Essays 1948*,
58-73. Ed. D. A. Robertson, Jr. New York: Columbia University Press,
1949.

Granville-Barker, Harley. Preface, *Twelfth Night, An Acting Edition*. London:
Heinemann, 1912.

Green, William. *Shakespeare's 'Merry Wives of Windsor.'* Princeton: Princeton
University Press, 1962.

Hotson, Leslie. *Shakespeare versus Shallow*. Boston: Little Brown, 1931.

—. *The First Night of Twelfth Night*. London: Heinemann [1954], repr. 1961.

Leggatt, Alexander. *Citizen Comedy in the Age of Shakespeare*. Toronto:
University of Toronto Press, 1973.

—. *Shakespeare's Comedy of Love*. London: Methuen, 1974.

Oliver, H. J., ed. Introduction, *The Merry Wives of Windsor*. New Arden
Shakespeare. London: Methuen, 1971.

Polanyi, Michael. *Personal Knowledge*. New York: Harper, 1964.

Welsford, Enid. *The Fool: His Social and Literary History*. London: Faber, 1935.

Whittaker, Herbert. "Full Shakespeare Texts Return – With Bonuses." *The
Globe and Mail*, Toronto, 11 August 1956.

(Play texts quoted are from the Penguin Shakespeare series, published by Penguin Books Ltd., Harmondsworth, England.)

All's Well That Ends Well, copyright © 1970; Introduction, copyright © Barbara Everett, 1970.

As You Like It, copyright © 1968; Introduction, copyright © H.J. Oliver, 1968.

Antony and Cleopatra, copyright © 1977; Introduction, copyright © Emrys Jones, 1977.

The Comedy of Errors, copyright © 1972; Introduction, copyright © Stanley Wells, 1972.

Coriolanus, copyright © 1967; Introduction, copyright © G.R. Hibbard, 1967.

Cymbeline, not yet in print.

Hamlet, copyright © 1980; Introduction, copyright © Anne Barton, 1980.

1 Henry IV, copyright © 1968; Introduction, copyright © P.H. Davison, 1968.

2 Henry IV, copyright © 1977; Introduction, copyright © P.H. Davison, 1977.

Henry V, copyright © 1968; Introduction, copyright © A.R. Humphreys, 1968.

1 Henry VI, copyright © 1981; Introduction, copyright © Norman Sanders, 1981.

2 Henry VI, copyright © 1981; Introduction, copyright © Norman Sanders, 1981.

3 Henry VI, copyright © 1981; Introduction, copyright © Norman Sanders, 1981.

Henry VIII, copyright © 1971; Introduction, copyright © A.R. Humphreys, 1971.

Julius Caesar, copyright © 1967; Introduction, copyright © Norman Sanders, 1967.

King John, copyright © 1974; Introduction, copyright © R.L. Smallwood, 1974.

King Lear, copyright © 1972; Introduction, copyright © G.K. Hunter, 1972.

Love's Labour's Lost, copyright © 1982; Introduction, copyright © John Kerrigan, 1982.

Macbeth, copyright © 1977; Introduction, copyright © G.K. Hunter, 1977.

Measure for Measure, copyright © 1969; Introduction, copyright © J.M. Nosworthy, 1969.

The Merchant of Venice, copyright © 1967; Introduction, copyright © W. Moelwyn Merchant, 1967.

The Merry Wives of Windsor, copyright © 1973; Introduction, copyright © G.R. Hibbard, 1973.

Much Ado About Nothing, copyright © 1978; Introduction, copyright © R.A. Foakes, 1978.

A Midsummer Night's Dream, copyright © 1967; Introduction copyright © Stanley Wells, 1967.